Life on the Bum in the Early 1930's

A Memoir

By

Allen Kussmaul

As told to

Joe R. Bula

authorHOUSE®

AuthorHouse™
1663 Liberty Drive, Suite 200
Bloomington, IN 47403
www.authorhouse.com
Phone: 1-800-839-8640

First published by AuthorHouse 4/21/2009

ISBN: 978-1-4389-5400-4 (sc)

Printed in the United States of America
Bloomington, Indiana

This book is printed on acid-free paper.

INTRODUCTION

My name is Allen Kussmaul. I have a tale I would like to share with you before my ninety-five years catch up to me. Yeah, I don't believe it either, 95, but I'm the one that's got to live with that fact. So, before this tale disappears into the clouds of my mind won't you sit a spell and let an old man share with you a memorable part of my life.

Writing memoirs is like inventing a time machine. Mine was set in 1931. I was 17 years old, 5 feet 8 inches, 135 pounds and going to be a senior in high school come next fall. I had made up my mind to spend the summer hiking around the United States. A time machine is like the old flivver Dad had in those days: I knew it was going to start eventually but I never knew if I was going to get by with just turning the key or was I going to have to crank until my arm almost fell off.

Telling my story has had some easy starts and other days I've had to crank. Some names have been changed to keep anyone's nose from getting too out of line and remember, this is how I remember it 75 years after it happened and not meant to be an autobiography full of boring facts.

When I told Dad my plans, he knew me well enough to know I was going and the amount of money I had really didn't matter to me. I was strong from the work around the farm and was not afraid of hard work. I had to go. He staked me $50 and gave me a money belt to keep it safely hidden under my shirt. Mom gave me food---oatmeal, raisins, cocoa, a couple sandwiches and cookies. My older brother Glen filled me with stories of his travels and lessons he had learned.

I left my home in Mt. Hope, Wisconsin on June 2, 1931 and returned August 3, with $13 to return to Dad. This is my tale of how I was able to visit 37 states at an average cost of $1 per state, besides being in Canada. It is a tale of police blockades, big fat egg sandwiches, dust storms and floods, heat so hot it burned my back through my shirt, and cold that kept me up all night tending a fire. I accepted rides from a prizefighter and a wrestler, a U.S. Senator and a cotton picker, a barber and a teacher, and many more I'll tell you about later. I saw museums and monuments, mountains and plains, swamps and deserts. I worked as a babysitter, night watchman, fruit picker, and driver. I fished and hunted. I rode in trucks, cars of all types, a motorcycle, a train, a buckboard and more Models T's than Henry Ford. I was given help and directions from little old ladies, truck drivers,

Uncles and aunts, Cajuns, Mexicans, darkeys, Texans and a U.S. Senator. I found a country crippled by the depression, split apart by prohibition and segregation, but working together, helping each other and struggling, not down and out. I found people from all over on the roads. Okies wanted to pick peaches in California, poor whites from the south wanted to build cars in Detroit, darkeys from Mississippi wanted to go up north and work in the factories or textile mills, and Swedes from Wisconsin going to work the oil fields of Texas. Everyone thought it was going to be better someplace else. It was the American way and I was in the middle of it.

That was why I started out, for the adventure. When someone travels today they expect it to be a trouble-free trip and may even get angry if it's not. In 1931 we expected travel to be full of trouble. That was the adventure of it. That is why I started out--for the adventure of it.

I am first going to write what I wrote in my diary in 1931. Then I'll follow it with some comments or memories I have had since I discovered the diary in my attic in January of 1991.

HOW I FOUND AMERICA IN 1931

April 17, 1931

Received this book today. Also received a packsack I intend to use this summer. We beat Lancaster baseball team 12 to 0. I am a junior in high school.

During the winter of my junior year in high school, I began thinking that more than anything I wanted to spend the summer hitchhiking around the United States. I was 17 years old when I received my new diary. A packsack made of waterproof canvas had also arrived from the mail order catalogue. I adjusted the two straps so it rested high on my shoulders and kept my hands free. A pair of hiking shoes would be added later.

"I want to see those shoes when you get back," said the salesman. I think he was just trying to drum up more business for later. It was the Great Depression and that meant a lot more than just a phrase in a book. If you were one of the lucky ones and had a job, brother, you'd do almost anything to keep it.

The depression was two years old by this time and money was scarce. But everyone was in the same boat; you aren't poor when everybody else is poor too. We lived off what the land produced and bought only necessary items. Jobs were scarce too, and especially for a 17 year-old boy. The older men with families needed the available jobs. I recorded in my diary that eggs were 11 cents a dozen but then a year later on April 30, 1932, eggs were 8 cents a dozen, butter 18 cents a pound, pork

3.5 cents a pound and lots of times there was no market for beef. All picture shows were 10 cents.

Monday, June 1, 1931

Packed my hiking outfit today. Getting ready to leave tomorrow. Lucile Stender started to work here. Rud started with George Engles at the County Farm to build a horse barn.

My packsack was chock-full and cumbersome. It must have weighed at least 50 pounds and contained a lightweight canvas; six feet by eight feet, a wool army blanket, canteen, two quart tin syrup pail, small frying pan, tin cup, plate, fork, fishing line wrapped around a cork and some hooks, a good pocket knife, camera, towel, an extra set of clothes, and other odds and ends. On the back of my packsack I attached a large triangle shaped banner with Wisconsin written on it. It helped me get rides more than once during the summer. Dad gave me fifty dollars in folding money. Most of it went into a money belt under my shirt, the rest into a leather pocket book with a clasp on top that I kept in my shirt pocket. That was a lot of money for those times. I felt like a walking millionaire.

Tuesday, June 2, 1931

Started on hike. Glen took me to Bridgeport. Crossed at Prairie and got as far as Emmetsburg, Iowa. Camped in a pasture. Ride getting was good. Helped load some wool.

So finally, I was leaving home. Months of preparation and worry and runaway excitement and now the trip was beginning. The weather was perfect for my first day of traveling. My brother Glen drove me to Bridgeport, about 15 miles from home, in the family's Model T Ford and I started to hitchhike across the narrow, two-way, covered wooded bridge. I was just getting used to the way my packsack rode on my shoulders and starting to worry about how I was going to manage if two cars met at the same time when my first ride picked me up and took me into Prairie du Chien. By the time I got there I was in bad need of a toilet. I stopped at Gagdon's filling station where he had an outside toilet. I leaned my packsack against the outside and went in. When I came out old man Gagdon was waiting for me and raked me over the coals good.

"I don't want every damn stinkin' bum in the country using my toilet." He said. "It's for customers only. You just get your damn packsack and get the hell out of here before I kick your ass to kingdom come."

I wanted to ask him if he didn't recognize me. "I'm Al Kussmaul, son of Rudolf Kussmaul of Mt. Hope. He's been a customer of yours all my life." But I remembered Dad telling me last night at supper, "This will be your first experience where people are going to judge you first by what you appear to be, second by what you do and there may even be a few who will get to know you well enough to know what you stand for. Just remember, they don't know or care who's your father or mother, or who your brothers are. They don't care if you know how to play baseball or how badly you beat Lancaster last spring. They are going to look at you for maybe five seconds and make up their minds about you. If people don't know you, you can't tell them, you're going to have to show them who you really are. Just remember that and learn how to use it and deal with it."

I could see now that my packsack made me look like a bum in some people's eyes and there wasn't anything I could do about changing their minds. I turned and walked away, smiling to myself as I could feel the money belt strapped around my chest and thinking how with that $50 in there I could be anybody I wanted to be.

That was my first good bawling out and it left me with a bad taste in my mouth for Gagdon's station for years to come. It's hard to say how many tanks of gas I could have bought from him over the next seventy years. He lost a lot of money that day.

I paid ten cents for a ferry ride across the Mississippi River over to McGregor, Iowa. While I was waiting for it to arrive from the other side, I bought a Gays Mills' apple from a man set up nearby the dock. It was last year's crop and had no doubt spent the winter in a barrel in his cellar. He had three separate piles set up on the ground in front of him. The first pile looked really good with no rotten spots and was priced at two cents each.

The second pile had a few bad spots I had to carve out with my pocketknife but it was worth the penny I paid for one. The third pile was two for a penny but it would have taken two to get enough good eaten as I already had in my one. You get what you pay for and it's not always the best or the most. But it was a real treat to have an apple to eat this time of the year. I enjoyed every bite and threw the trimmings and the core into the cocoa colored Mississippi current and watched them float downriver towards New Orleans. Maybe I would beat them there.

The ferry carried cars and passengers headed west on Highway 18. The climb out of town on the steep winding road up to the bluffs that overlooked the river was the first real test I had of how my packsack was going to ride. The straps that seemed okay at home now cut into my shoulders causing a dull ache. I leaned my body into the weight and kept my head down with each step but each step seemed more like climbing stairs instead of hiking a road. With the passing of each car or truck I would stick out my thumb only to receive a wave in return. The dust kicked up by their passing would gag me for a moment and then settle on down. There was nothing for me to do but continue on up the steep river bluff road. I began to wonder if the whole world was like old man Gagdon and hated anyone with a packsack. Was I going to have to hike the whole trip? Finally, as I approached the top of the bluff where there was a turnout beside the road I noticed an old staked-rack truck with a couple bundles of wool in the bed. The driver's side door was open and

I could see half of a man sitting on the seat with one boot resting on the running board. He was wearing bib overalls, blue work shirt, and a straw hat. His arm muscles were huge compared to the rest of his body. He spit tobacco juice next to the truck and yelled back to me.

"I've been waiting for you to get up here. I saw you back there about a mile but the grade was so steep I was afraid my brakes wouldn't hold long enough to pick you up and if they did I wasn't sure I would be able to get going again. I've seen men wait all day long half way up that steep grade for a ride that couldn't stop if it wanted to. You're a smart man to keep on hiking to the top. Most times, where you are has a lot to do with whether you get a ride or not. The ride needs to be able to stop."

"Thanks for the advice. I'll sure keep that in mind during my travels."

I slipped off my pack and let it rest on the ground at my feet while I took a drink from my canteen. As I tipped my head back my shoulders and back rejoiced at their relaxed freedom. It felt good to hear him call me a man and not a boy or kid. I liked what I heard.

"A man sure needs a drink after a climb like you just made."

"Looks like your truck does too." I answered while I pointed my canteen toward its steaming radiator.

"You're right there." He said with a chugging laugh. The kind that sounds like a steam locomotive just getting started. Releasing the laugh from deep in his chest and letting it blast out his mouth. "I got its own personal water jug sitting here on the floorboards just waiting for it to quit blowing off steam so I can give it the cool drink it needs. Where you headed?"

"Don't know for sure. Left Mt. Hope this morning and am starting out to see these United States. I want to learn how people are doing before I start my senior year of high school next fall. I'll just let my next ride tell me where I'm going and see what happens. Maybe California, maybe Texas, who knows?"

"Well, you're welcome to ride a spell with me if you want. I'm headed for Postville with a few stops in between. Got some wool to pick up and sure could use some help loading, if you're willing."

I told him that sounded great to me and loaded my packsack in the rear of the truck, glad to be rid of it for awhile. We filled the radiator with water and soon were bouncing off down the dirty, rutted road.

"Know how to read a spring scale?" He asked.

"Yah, sure. We use them around the farm all the time."

"Well, then here's what we'll do. I'll hang the spring scale on the side of the truck and you'll hang the wool on it and call out the weight on the scale. I'll write it down and tally them up, settle up with the farmer and then we'll stack them in the truck. Sound fair enough?"

I found that if a farmer sheared his sheep correctly the wool was so thick that it would stick together in a bundle and all that was needed was some string to hold it together. I could use the string to hang the bundles on the spring scale.

The first farmer we bought wool from, the buyer stated his price per pound and settled up with the farmer in quick order and we were on our way. However, the next farmer we came to had his own scale and hung it on the truck next to our scale. The difference in the scales was noted with the first bundle and an average correction agreed upon. After all bundles were weighed, the price per pound stated by the buyer was lower than what it had been with the previous farmer. The bargaining began. After 5 minutes of bickering back and forth a price was finally agreed upon that turned out to be the same price per pound as the first farmer. He paid the farmer and we loaded the truck.

"I noticed you offered that farmer less for his wool than the first one. Is there that much difference in the quality of wool around here?"

"Naw, the wool is pretty much all the same. But in this business, or any other business, you have to know your customer and know what they expect. You see the first farmer trusted me. He knew from doing business with me over the past 10 years that I was not going to cheat him. My price has always been fair. However, I knew the second farmer was going to want to bargain. He's always wanted to get a better price than what I offered. So, I knew how much of a better price he wanted and started him out that much lower. It's important to know your customer and to know they are going to talk among themselves when you leave. You don't have to treat everyone the same but you have to treat everyone fairly. Don't ever cheat anyone, not even yourself. Offer a fair price and make a fair profit and you'll stay in business a long time."

We unloaded his truck in a warehouse in Postville and he gave me a ride to the edge of town where it was easy for my next ride to stop and pick me up.

Postville was as far west as I had ever been, so from then on I was in new territory. I felt I was entering a mystery. Like Alice in Wonderland I had stepped through the magic mirror. I had prepared myself but I wasn't cocky enough to think there weren't challenges ahead. Big, big challenges. But I didn't have a clue about what would happen. I prayed I would stay healthy and strong. I knew I was going to need it.

After getting short rides, I was walking for a spell when the smell of fresh baked bread reminded me that I was getting hungry. My nose turned me in the direction of a newly whitewashed two-story farmhouse with a red barn set back off the road. A deeply rutted lane led up to the house. Grazing sheep and chickens were drinking from the muddy pools formed in the ruts by last night's rain or were lazily keeping the grass short around the house and lane. They raised their heads at my approach, adjusted their position to maintain a safe distance and returned to their grazing. Two rocking chairs beckoned from the front porch, moving slightly in the afternoon breeze. "Not now," I thought. "Not now. I have a sandwich to find somewhere around here." And I knew a stranger always goes to the back door, it was just good country manners.

I noticed a woodshed located near the rear of the house as I stepped up to the rear door, knocked, and asked the lady if I could do some work for a sandwich. She showed me the woodpile and axe and said, "You split some stove wood while I get the bread out of the oven and fix you a sandwich."

Well, I was used to work and splitting wood was right up my alley, but I soon found out that this woodpile was all willow wood. It didn't split easy like the oak I was used to and I pounded my fool head off for a half-hour or more. The lady seemed well satisfied, handed me two sandwiches in a paper bag and asked me if I didn't want to stay longer because her husband could use good help around the farm.

"No thanks, Ma'am. I'll be moving on but I would like to fill my canteen at your well if I could."

"Sure, help yourself."

The pump was being driven by a windmill and was over by the barn and livestock pens. It creaked and groaned like an old man getting up from a nap, as its blades turned in the wind and the long pump rod lowered and raised. With each up stroke came a splash of water out of the spigot that ran down a long pipe and into a wooden stock tank in the empty pen as the cattle could be seen in the distant pasture. I almost peeled off my shirt but I remembered my money belt and just dunked my head into the cool, refreshing water in the tank. It felt so good. I grabbed my canteen out of my pack, emptied it on the ground and filled it with the fresh water spilling out of the pipe. I wiped my face with my shirtsleeve, put one of the two homemade bread-and-egg sandwiches, made with fresh churned butter, into my pack next to some grub I was saving that Mother had sent along. Then I hooked up my canteen, slipped into my pack straps and strolled down the road eating the other sandwich. I couldn't have been happier.

Sunset found me west of Emmetsburg, Iowa. I found a small stream where I made my first camp about 100 yards off the road, behind some brush in a pasture. I built a fire between a couple stones, cooked up a bucket of cocoa and ate my other sandwich for supper. Then I spread my bed on the ground by laying out the canvas, then the blanket, took off my shoes, left my clothes on, laid on half, and pulled the other half of the canvas and blanket over me like a butterfly waiting to be born. I used my pack as a pillow. This kept me dry in case rain would come up in the night.

Wednesday, June 3, 1931

Rode nearly all day with a young man from California. From Iowa to St. Cloud, Minnesota. Tire trouble. Went through a sandstorm. Got to St. Cloud at 10 o'clock. Hiked two miles out and slept in a field.

The first thing I did each morning was fix breakfast. I brought oatmeal and raisins along, and condensed milk in a small can. I cooked up the oatmeal using water from my canteen and my two-quart tin pail. I would mix a little of the condensed milk with water in my cup and then add it to my oatmeal. I also carried a little bag of sugar to add to the oatmeal. Put it all together with my cocoa and I started my day with quite a feast. I whittled a little wooden plug for the hole I had poked in the condensed milk can and then packed it away carefully in my mess kit before putting it away in my pack. I used the whole can before it spoiled and bought more when I needed to.

I thought I was a long way from home when I started my second day of hitchhiking. I didn't have any definite route to follow and at the time thought I might head west to California. I was taking a break at a crossroad and was just getting ready to throw a clump of grass into the air and go whatever direction the wind blew it when a man in a Model T stopped.

"Where you headed?" He asked.

"Don't matter to me, maybe California."

"I just came from California. Nothing out there for a working man. I'm headed up to St. Cloud, Minnesota. You ever been there?"

"No, but I'm game to go along if you want me."

"Hop in."

I threw my packsack in the rear seat and climbed into the front seat. We got three or four miles down the road and the old flivver started bucking and bouncing something terrible.

"Feels like we got a flat tire." Said the driver.

We climbed out of the car and sure enough, we had a flat and two of the other three tires were going down fast. There wasn't anything to do but fix them. They all had bare spots where I could see the tread was worn completely through and the cords sticking out. It didn't look like they could last another mile. As the driver went to his toolbox on the running board, I noticed his toolbox was bigger than his suitcase. That should have told me something. He grabbed out a screw jack and a couple of tire irons. We jacked up the wheels one at a time, peeled the tires off the rims with the two tire irons, cut patches out of an old tube he had thrown in the backseat, glued on the patch, and worked on another tire while the patch dried. We installed the tube into the tire and pried it back on the rim with the tire irons, being careful not to pinch the repaired tube. We pumped them up with a leaky hand pump, unscrewed the jack, and then we were ready to start the motor and head on down the road.

Now this old Tin Lizzy was no angel to start. First he leaned in over the steering wheel and set the spark and throttle levers like that of the hands of a clock at ten minutes to three. Then he walked around to the front of the car and grabbed the crank that stuck out from under the radiator. He seized the crank in his right hand carefully, for the Model T's were famous for kicking back and causing broken arms or sprained wrists. He slipped his left forefinger through a loop of wire that controlled the choke. He pulled the loop of wire, and spun the crank mightily by pulling upward. Repeated this action until the engine at last roared. He then pushed the choke wire back, leaped onto the trembling running board, leaned in and moved the spark and throttle to twenty-five minutes to two, and then jumped in and slipped down behind the steering wheel with the engine running the way it should. He then released the handbrake lever, pressed down on the left of the three pedals on the floor. This started the car moving forward in low gear, releasing the pedal put it in high and we were off down the road, increasing our speed by pulling downward on the throttle lever. The center pedal was reverse and the right foot pedal was the brake.

I learned my driver was a barber by trade. He knew someone in St. Cloud and hoped to stay with him while he looked for a job. It was like that all over the country. It seemed like half of the people were looking for work and the other half was willing to help them find it. I told him he could have cut my hair but Mom had just cut it the day before I left, just two days ago.

He told me a little secret about barbershops. The barber in the first chair was the one with the most experience and was most expensive---20 cents to 25 cents per haircut. The next barber was less experienced and less expensive---15 cents to 20 cents. And the one farthest back was the least experienced and cheapest---10 cents to 15 cents. You get what you pay for, is what he told me and I have found that to be true about almost anything. Although I notice most barbershops are busiest in the back.

About noontime we noticed the road disappeared just ahead of us. Soon we could see it was a huge cloud of dust rolling our way. It surrounded us and blinded us so we couldn't see the road. We slowed way down and finally had to stop or take a chance of driving off the road and getting stuck in the ditch. It was worse than getting caught in a snowstorm. We closed our eyes to keep out the sand. We covered our mouths and noses with our hands and when that didn't work we climbed under the car and pulled our shirts over our heads and breathed through the cloth. I thought we were about to suffocate and there was nothing we could do about it. I could feel the fine, powdered dust sifting into my ears, my armpits and into my pants around my belt. We tried to drive on but couldn't see the edge of the road. Finally, it was gone. The air cleared up and we could see and breathe again. We dusted ourselves off and headed out where we thought the road should be. Sometimes we had to bust through drifts of dirt that had piled up across the road.

There were lots of jackrabbits in this part of the country. They were in the fields eating what was left of the crops or alongside the roads. He had to swerve a couple of times to avoid running over them. Then late in the afternoon he reached under his seat and pulled out a big, long revolver and handed it to me.

"Here, shoot one of those rabbits and we'll cook him up for supper."

Well, I had enjoyed hunting around the farm with a 22 rifle for several years and had shot my share of rabbits and squirrels but this was the first time I had ever fired a revolver. By the time we picked out a jack to shoot, stopped the car and I lay across the hood to steady my aim, the jack would be off. I shot three or four times without hitting anything before we gave up on supper for that night.

We arrived in St. Cloud about ten o'clock. He left me off near his friend's house and I hiked out of town to a big signboard and made camp in a pasture nearby. Some hot cocoa and a can of beans sure tasted good.

Thursday, June 4, 1931

Rode in back of an old fashioned truck from St. Cloud to Ferguson Falls. Got ride with a schoolteacher to Ada. Surprised the Key family. Stayed all night with them. Went through the Red River Lake bottom.

Rides were pretty hard to come by up there so I was glad to see this old fashioned truck come along. It had hard rubber tires on what looked to be old wagon wood-spoked wheels. There was just room enough up front for the driver so I threw my packsack in the back and climbed up with it. The road was too bumpy to let me lie down in the truck and there was nothing to sit on except my packsack, so I ended up standing all the way up to Ferguson Falls, Minnesota. I was glad when the driver said that was as far as he was going that day. I hiked out of town a few miles and then caught a ride with a schoolteacher up to Ada and the Key family farm.

The schoolteacher was bound for Grand Forks to look for work. His school had closed due to lack of students. In this area many of the parents couldn't afford to send their kids to school because they had been unable to sell their crops. The schools stayed open but expected the teachers to work for next to nothing or for whatever the parents would send with their kids.

This teacher hoped the bigger towns would have more money but he had heard that other teachers felt the same way and he expected to find 100 teachers had applied for the same job.

The Fitz Key family had been our next door neighbors back in Mt. Hope. The year before, they had moved up to a farm near Ada, Minnesota. Boy, were they surprised to see me. They fed me up good, let me take a bath and sleep in a real bed for a change. They had a nice place and were working hard.

Friday, June 5, 1931

Went from Ada to Lakota, North Dakota. Passed through Grand Forks. Slept in a grove of trees. Pretty cold. Thinly settled country. An old couple picked me up on the street in Crookston, Minnesota and took me to Grand Forks.

It was leaving Ada that I found out this hitchhiking was mostly hiking. Rides were hard to come by because this was thinly settled country and they were having hard times. I saw many abandoned farms with the buildings going to ruin and the land to weeds. The Key family told me many farmers sold their livestock for next to nothing just to keep from starving. I passed by many grain elevators filled with wheat, which no one had the money to buy. It took a long time for me to get to Cookston and while I was resting by the street trying to decide what to do next an old couple picked me up and offered to take me to Grand Forks with them. I was glad to get any ride I could and I took them up on their offer.

"I don't see why anyone would want to go west from here." Said the old lady. "You'll starve to death out there on the prairies. There just aren't any people out there and it's miles between towns. Not many cars or trucks for rides either. If I was you I'd head south where the roads are better and there are more people to help you out."

"I was kind of thinking about going to California."

"Well, you better go south first. You'll die going west from here."

They fed me a good meal at Grand Forks and took me to the edge of town and I started hiking from there. I had hiked all the way to Lakota, about 20 miles, with only one short ride when I decided to make camp in the only grove of trees just outside of town.

I have always remembered that night very well. It was the coldest night I put in. After building a fire and cooking up my supper I made my bed on the ground and in a few hours I was really cold. I put my boots back on but they were cold too and I built a small fire to try and warm up. I tried to make a tent out of my canvas so as to get the benefit of the fire but the smoke would get so thick I would have to take it down in order to breathe. I sat as close to the fire as I could and still stay out of the smoke, then I would doze off a little only to wake when the fire was almost out. I'd add sticks to the fire to keep it going and try again to get a few winks of sleep.

I had it all figured out by morning. I abandoned my expectations. I was finished heading west and I would now head south so I could warm up.

Saturday, June 6, 1931

Cold night, started back to Grand Forks to go south. Caught a 300-mile ride down to Graceville, Min. Caught more rides to Summit, South Dakota. Went through Wet Stone Valley. Slept in a schoolhouse.

I backtracked my highway to Grand Forks and caught a 300-mile ride down to Graceville, Minnesota. That put me south quite a ways. I went over into South Dakota in order to get a good road going south.

Somewhere along the road in South Dakota a car stopped and a large man got out. He was wearing a pair of old scuffed boots, coveralls with patches on both knees, a blue denim shirt with curly hairs bristling out the top. His unshaven face had an unlit cigar stub shoved over to one corner of a yellow tooth stained mouth that peeked out from under a bushy mustache and his tattered straw hat was shoved down to his ears while holding on against the wind.

"Get in. I got some hay I need put up." He said.

"But I'm not looking for a job. I'm just looking for a ride south." I replied.

"My place is just about three miles south of here. I got twenty acres of hay I need put up right away. It shouldn't take more than two or three days. Now get in the car."

I had heard and read stories about how men had been forced to work against their will. Sailors were knocked out only to wake up on a ship far out to sea, boys and girls were kidnapped to work in homes as servants or workers. I was worried this big man would force me into his car and make me work for him. I looked around to see where I could run. There was no one to help me for miles around. If I ran I would have to leave my packsack behind.

"You must think I'm broke and looking for work but I don't want a job. I'm just traveling around the country to look it over."

"What you mean you don't want no job?"

He started toward me. One of his big, callused, dirty hands reached out. I backed away, leaving my packsack behind and looking over my shoulder, getting ready to run.

"You must be a good for nothing bum if you won't work when a job is offered. I've never laid eyes on a lazier muttenhead in my life than what you are. I hope you rot out here on this road and the buzzards carry you off before you can catch another ride."With that said, he got into his car and threw gravel at me with his spinning rear tires. I watched him disappear over the next hill and then looked around. I was relieved I didn't see any buzzards in the sky and that he was gone out of my life.

I kept on hiking until toward evening I came upon a little red, one-room, country schoolhouse. I didn't know about hereabouts but at home I knew the school door was never locked. They figured it was better to leave the door open so that a thief could get in and see there wasn't anything to steal than to lock it up and have to repair it after someone broke in. It also gave travelers somewhere to go in case they got stranded in bad weather or something. I thought I would give this old school a try and sure enough, it was open. There was a nice woodstove inside and a hand-pump well outside, so I knew I had it made for the night. I went on in, warmed up a can of beans and cocoa on the woodstove and dipped some of Mom's rolls in it for supper.

There was a metal bucket out by the well so I used that to warm up some water and was able to wash off some of the smoke smell I had become so attached to the night before. My clothes still smelled badly but at least I felt better. I spread my bedroll between the teacher's desk and the blackboard and had a good night's sleep.

Sunday, June 7, 1931

Picked up by two young men from Wis. Started on our way to Oklahoma with them. They were nearly broke and I pretended I was. Tried to sell their car. Saw a flood and tornado area. We were traveling about eleven o'clock at night and we thought we were being held up. They were lawmen, pulled guns on us and made us stop. Camped at Norfolk, Nebraska.

The next morning I caught a ride into Summit, South Dakota. As I walked toward the outskirts I heard someone yell at me.

"Hey, Wisconsin badger, where ya going?" I turned to see who was doing the yelling and saw two young, blonde-haired men standing next to a Model T Ford and talking to a man in a business suit.

"I'm heading south. Just out here looking the country over. What are you guys doing?"

"We see from that banner on your pack, you must be from Wisconsin. We're from Wisconsin too, Cambridge. Ever heard of it?"

Now I had never heard of Cambridge, Wisconsin but I knew that if I could keep these guys talking they would tell me all about it and they might even be able to help me along with my travels. I was right on both counts.

"Sure, hasn't everyone heard of Cambridge? What're you doing here?"

"Well, we're out of money and food. So we're trying to sell our car to this man here but he doesn't want to give us anything for it. A good car like this in such good shape ought to be worth at least $100 but this man only wants to give us $10. It's a crying shame how people try to take advantage of people when they're down and out. I've a good notion to give this nice salesman standing next to me another 5 minutes to make up his mind and if he doesn't come up with the $100 he knows this car is worth, we'll just give you a ride south. We are headed for Oklahoma anyway."

"Well, you boys have a nice trip in that nice car." Said the salesman, as he walked away.

"Well, I got enough food for at least one meal in my pack and I just passed a bakery up the street where we can get some more rolls. If you boys are really serious, I'd sure take you up on that offer of a ride to Oklahoma." I replied quickly before they changed their minds and sold their car.

I discovered earlier that it was possible to go into a bakery and ask for a dime's worth of old rolls. That usually meant I could get a big brown bag full of old sweet rolls, hard rolls or even a loaf of bread or two. Old rolls were better than fresh because they kept better in my packsack and when I soaked them in cocoa or water they were good eating. I got the rolls and some more canned beans, and used another fifty cents to get a tank of gas. I paid out of my pocketbook and let on that I was almost broke too.

We stopped in the town park just long enough to share a couple cans of beans and the bag of rolls. They told me their names were Hans Rudd and Hans Anderson.

"Well now, that won't work at all." I said. "I have a brother named Rudd, so I'll call you Rudd and Andy seems like a good name for anyone named Anderson. If that won't make you boys mad it would sure make it easier on me."

"That sounds fair enough to us." Rudd answered for both of them.

The old Model T would run but that was about all that could be said for it. They had a gallon can of used motor oil they had begged off the station owner where we bought the gas and had filled a five gallon can with water for the radiator. We headed out of town, southbound.

Somewhere between Summit and the Missouri River near Yankton, South Dakota, we passed through an area that a tornado had devastated. Everything was scattered. The cottonwood trees were either blown over sideways or had been stripped of their leaves and small branches and their tops were snapped off. They stood there like wooden giants with stubby arms, trunks with a few large limbs. Many of the buildings were leveled and people picked through the piles of junk that had been their homes or farm buildings. Windmills were broken in half or had most of their blades missing. I saw one cow bawling over a dead calf that had a board stuck in its side. All people saved were a few cans of food and some pictures or photo albums. Stock tanks were filled with debris and the cattle wouldn't go near them. Branches, corn stalks, and grass hung from the wire fences like clothes put out to dry. We stopped several times to clear away trees that had blown across the road. We found some canned food to add to our supplies but then gave it to a family that was sitting next to their storm cellar where they had hidden while the storm blew away their home and barn. All they had left was one milk cow and a few chickens running around loose. They were pretty shook up but vowed to rebuild and start over.

"I still have what's left of my wheat crop in the field. It's been blown flat but I think we can salvage some of it. We have to." Said the man. "And besides, where would I go anyway? My families all here. They'll all help and the folks from the church have already been over with food and to ask what else we're going to need. I know they'll give me the help I'd give them if things were reversed."

I sure hope he gets enough rain for a bumper crop. I thought. He'll need every penny of it. But I sure admired his grit.

Later that day we crossed over the Missouri River near Yankton. The area had been flooded recently. We saw whole farms destroyed. Years of hard work, crops, and buildings were gone. The stench was terrible. Decaying livestock and crops were everywhere. In places the road had been washed away and we had to detour across the fields until we hooked back up with it. The approaches to the bridges had been washed away but had been repaired enough so that we were able to get across.

We were sure glad to get into Nebraska. Being broke didn't seem like anything when compared to the suffering I saw in these poor people.

We decided to drive all night to make up for the time we had lost going through the tornado and flood areas. We took turns driving. At about 11 o'clock, we came around a curve in the road and found it blocked by two cars parked across from ditch to ditch. We came to a stop and there were men on both sides of our car shining flashlights into the windows. I was sure it was a hold up and stuffed my pocketbook into the top of one of my socks.

"Get out of the car so we can get a look at you." Someone shouted in the darkness. As I climbed out of the car I could see men holding shotguns and some had handguns stuck in their belts or in holsters. I tried not to let them see how I was shaking. I tried to put my hands in my pockets but someone yelled for us to put our hands up. We did. I suddenly had to pee. It was worse than I had ever experienced. I couldn't think of anything else but what a fool these men would make of me if I peed my pants. I squeezed everything I could think of to hold it in. My fists clenched, my teeth ground together and my knees were pinched tight.

"Where you boys from?"

"Wisconsin." Answered Rudd.

"What you doing out here driving at night?"

"We got jobs waiting for us in the Oklahoma oil fields. We are taking turns driving and sleeping."

"Hey Sheriff, here's a packsack in the back seat with a Wisconsin banner sewed on it. Looks like they're telling the truth." Someone yelled out of the darkness near the rear of the car.

My packsack was thrown on the ground and lights were shone on it. The man they called Sheriff started poking around it a little. I saw his badge clipped to his vest and I started feeling better. At least we weren't going to be held up.

"You boys, get loaded up and keep on going down the road. Don't look back." He said. "Okay, get those cars out of the way."

We didn't say anything. I grabbed my packsack, threw it in the backseat and climbed in with it. Rudd and Andy got in the front seat.

"Can you guys give us a little push, please?" Rudd asked.

After a short push, he engaged the clutch lever, the motor rolled over, backfired once, and scared the hell out of everyone. I hit the floor expecting the car to be filled with bullets from the Sheriff's posse and stayed there while Rudd put it at full throttle. We were at least a mile away before he stopped the car and we all scrambled out to pee in the ditch and each took a deep breath before we started to laugh uncontrollably.

"Boy, am I glad you had that banner on your pack." Said Andy. "No way of telling how long they would have kept us there if they hadn't seen that. I would have peed my pants for sure. I've never been so scared in my life."

We never learned who or what those men were looking for but were sure glad to get away from there. That stop kept us all wide awake until we got into Norfolk, Nebraska where we found a park on the edge of town and slept next to the car.

Monday, June 8, 1931

We started on with a full tank of gas and 17 cents. Tried four places to pawn his watch. Pawned it at a filling station for six dollars. Camped at McPherson, Kansas. Bought eggs and cooked them for supper. Tried fishing in the Platte River.

That next morning we were again faced with a near empty gas tank. Andy tried four different places to pawn his watch and finally found a man at a Standard Oil gas station that agreed to give him $6 and a tank of gas. I let them know I only had 17 cents left in my pocket book and didn't let on that I had anymore.

Now those old gas stations were something to behold too. We would tell the owner how much gas we wanted to buy and pay him. He would hand pump the gas up into the glass top that measured the amount with marks painted on the glass. Usually we would get about 5 gallons at a cost of 10 to 12 cents a gallon. After he pumped the amount into the glass he would place the nozzle into our gas tank which was located under the front seat and the gas would run in by gravity and empty the glass container on the pump.

With a full tank of gas we headed south until we came to the Platte River. The boys decided they wanted to go swimming and wash their clothes, which were getting pretty rank by this time. I didn't want to take off my shirt, as I didn't want my traveling companions to see my money belt. So, I told them I would try a little fishing. I had taken along a cork with line wrapped around it and some miscellaneous fishhooks. I found a nice strong branch from a nearby willow tree and disappeared around a curve in the river. After I was sure I was out of sight I stripped down to my shorts, went for a little swim, and washed my clothes too. I put them back on wet and fished until I heard the boys calling for me. By that time the hot prairie wind had almost dried my clothes and I waded up to the boys through the shallow river and they were too busy teasing me about not catching anything to notice my clothes were damp.

By evening time we were near McPherson, Kansas and had already made up our minds that we were going to stop and not try to drive all night. They knew I still had 17 cents in my pocketbook, so I bought a dime bag of old rolls at the bakery and a dozen eggs for 7 cents. We camped just outside of town and cooked up a real feed---four eggs apiece, enough rolls to get stuffed, and some cocoa to wash it all down.

We had a good time traveling together and were lucky not to have had any car trouble. I told the boys how I stopped at farms along the way and saved up sandwiches. They thought that sounded like a good idea but agreed it would be pretty hard on a farmer if all three of us stopped at once. We agreed to split up the next day and see what happened. My having no money left in my pocketbook might have influenced their thinking. Anyway, I was looking forward to being alone again.

Tuesday, June 9, 1931

Got to Pond Creek, Oklahoma with them. Left them and started on. Rode with a prizefighter. Slept in a wheat field. They are starting to cut wheat. Tried to make camp but too many ants. Camped by Kingfisher.

My companions headed west from Pond Creek, Oklahoma. They knew someone out there and thought they could find work.

I rode with a prizefighter for a ways, a big man, bigger than most men I had seen. He said he had lost most of his fights because the pay was about the same. If he could get a little man to fight him it was better because people just loved to see a big man lose to a little man. "It's just in people's blood that way." He said. He could draw big crowds because people would go hungry to see one man beat up on another. He didn't figure he was ever going to be out of work. "My nose has been broke so many times that if a fly lands on it, it starts bleeding." He laughed.

On my way through Oklahoma I saw many wheat fields being cut and shocked. The first camp I made I soon found out the ground was covered with ants. So, I went out in a wheat field and put several shocks together and had a very comfortable night.

Wednesday, June 10, 1931

Walked a long ways. Split wood for some sandwiches. Got to a cotton area, also oil wells. Southern Oklahoma is a red soil. Very dirty traveling. Camped in a ravine by a cotton field 23 miles from Texas near Ryan.

The wheat fields had given way to grazing plains and that was all I could see for miles around. All the roads were gravel and really hot, dirty and dusty. I once again found this hitchhiking was mostly hiking. The difference here was that I could see a car or truck coming from a much greater distance. I would spot a big cloud of dust on the horizon and get all excited about maybe a ride was coming. Wait 5 or 10 minutes for it to get to me, eat dust for 2 or 3 minutes as it roared on by, and then pick up my packsack, dust myself off and keep on walking until the next cloud of dust broke the horizon.

I came upon a dilapidated house with a shed out back. I noticed a pile of wood behind the shed and thought I could maybe turn it into a sandwich or two. The house looked like it hadn't been painted in 10 years. There was no equipment or livestock around. Four or five layer hens were pecking in the grassless yard with their laying-boxes nailed to the side of the shed. An old skeleton thin dog watched as I went around to the rear door and knocked on the broken and ripped screen door only half expecting someone to answer. But a fine looking young lady answered my knock almost immediately.

"Well, what sorry gust of wind blew you in?" She asked.

"Good day ma'am." I stepped back surprised and answered. "I was just passin' through and wonder if I could split some wood for a cool drink and a sandwich." I guess I must have looked pretty sorry. I felt like I was carrying an extra inch of dust stuck all over my body. The bandanna I had over my mouth and nose must have made me look like an outlaw.

"Sure, sit down and I'll get some milk for you to drink and some water to wash that face of yours so I can see if you're really as ugly as you look like you might be. The well dried up and I have to haul water from a hole we dug down in the creek about half a mile away. It's good water though, once it settles out a little."

"Thank you, I sure could use a drink. Then I'll get right on that pile of wood out there."

She fixed me up with a drink of milk in a quart fruit jar. It was still thick with cream and helped coat my dry throat as it went down. Then I went out and tore into that woodpile. While I was splitting wood I got to thinking about home. How we just take our well, barnyard, garden and livestock for granted. They sure had a lower standard of living around here. The lady's garden plot was all dried up and I couldn't blame her if she had to haul water from half a mile away. The few chickens didn't look like they were being fed anything but just scratching around for what bugs they could find.

When I heard her call from the house, I quit splitting and went back to the rear door. I took off my bandana and wiped my face clean with my own sweat.

The lady had put a small table and chair outside near the door and had another tall glass of milk sitting next to a plate with a big egg sandwich on it. The bread slices were at least an inch thick.

"Thank you ma'am. Thank you very much." I sat down and started to enjoy."Where you from?" She asked while standing in the doorway and speaking through the broken screen door.

"I'm from Wisconsin. We have a family farm in southwest Wisconsin."

"Are farmers having a hard time up there too? Is that what you're doing out here looking for a job?"

"No, no, I'm not looking for a job. I'm just out here to see the country before I go back this fall and finish my senior year in high school. I'm just curious to see how people are doing."

"Well, we're having a hard time around here. It's been so dry that there hasn't been much of a cotton crop. What we did get to come up, the boll weevils ate. If it weren't for the little bit of wheat we got this year, we'd be starving. Thank goodness we can eat the wheat and feed a little bit of it to our chickens. That way we have bread, eggs and a little bit of milk that old Mollie can give us. Poor old milk cow has cleaned out about every blade of grass there is in our pasture. It's hard to grow her more grass when we can't get no rain. They been tryin' to get us to quit growin' cotton and plant peanuts or something else but growin' cotton is all we know. Wouldn't know what to do with peanuts if we did raise 'em."

"It's been hard, let me tell you. I don't know if we can last another dry year. My husband, right now, is in town pawnin' our wedding rings so we can get parts to fix the pump and dig the well deeper. Can't even sell the cotton. Nobody wants to buy it for a fair price. Ain't nobody got any money. There's talk around that even the bank might close. Don't make us no difference. We ain't got no money in there anyway. I just don't know what we're gonna to do."

She gazed off into the distance while she rubbed the white band on her left ring finger where her wedding band used to be. I think I saw a small tear form in the corner of one of her eyes as she focused on distant thoughts.

I didn't know what to tell her. It sure looked like a hard life. I figured they probably needed to rotate the crops like we did in Wisconsin but it didn't sound to me like she was interested in hearing me say something like that. I kept my mouth shut and thanked her for the good sandwich. When she came out with two more I tried to talk her into keeping them for herself and her husband but she insisted I take them. I tramped on down the road feeling sorry for her. My packsack had never felt heavier.

A little further down the road I passed by a tumbledown shack in the middle of what looked like a bean field. There were a couple of darkey kids playing with a dirty puppy on the front porch. I thought to myself that these darkeys sure must like beans to have a whole field full of them. I found out later it was a cotton field and boy did I ever feel stupid.

I camped in a ravine, by a cotton field, 23 miles from Texas near Ryan, Oklahoma. When I took my shirt off that night I found my back and shoulders were sunburned right through my shirt. Boy, was I sore.

Thursday, June 11, 1931

Woke up and heard darkeys singing while hoeing cotton. Passed over the Red River. Was helped through Fort Worth. Was afraid of cops. Went over plains and am striking trees. Camped in a meadow.

The darkeys were singing when I woke up. To what tune, I don't know, but they had their own song and kept time with their hoes. Men, women and kids were all working in the cotton field. They were out early before it got too hot to work.

I passed over the Red River just south of Ryan, Oklahoma. I thought I might stop and fish for awhile but it was almost dried up and very hot, so I kept on moving. I passed through oil fields in this area of Oklahoma and North Texas. It appeared there were thousands of people employed in the oil business. They constructed huge rigs just to drill in hopes of finding oil. Then when they found it they pumped it into large storage tanks next to the road and tanker trucks came along and transported it to the refineries. The spilled oil on the roads helped hold down the dust some and made for more pleasant hiking.

Just north of Fort Worth a man picked me up and told me the cops in Fort Worth were really tough on bums coming through. He was nice enough to take me clear through before he left me off. I was thankful for that. I had never had any run-ins with cops before my hike but that night in Nebraska with the boys had me spooked. I began to look on the cops as the enemy and didn't like being treated like a criminal just because I walked and carried a packsack.

I hiked on and caught a few short rides across the open range south of Ft. Worth and was starting to get back into country with a few trees when I made my camp for the night in a meadow.

Friday, June 12, 1931

Walked 14 miles before I caught a ride in a truck to San Antonio. Got there at 9:30 o'clock. Left the truck on outskirts and had to walk through alleys to find a hotel. Gave $2 for a room. Washed my clothes in the bath tub.

Rides were hard to come by and I hiked 14 miles before I caught a ride into San Antonio. He left me off on the outskirts of town at 9:30. I had to walk through a rough part of town to find a hotel.

It was Friday night so everyone was in a mood for a party. It was too hot to party inside and so everyone was in the streets. I didn't care anything about partying. I just wanted to find someplace to bed down for the night. I started looking for a park.

The first park I came to was full of partygoers. Everyone called me "Gringo" and spoke something about their sister and then they all would laugh. I didn't like the way they laughed at me, and how much fun they were having as they sent their dogs out to bark at me and follow me down the street. The little children would come out and grab at my packsack, laugh and shout, "Gringo, gringo."

Finally, I found what looked like a hotel. It was painted red with black trim. On the covered front porch men sat around tables playing cards, dominoes, or just drinking beer or some clear liquid from tall glasses. Light bulbs painted with red paint lit my way into the lobby and up to the desk. The man behind the counter looked me up and down and then shook his head and hand at me. "No Gringo," he said, "No room, no room." And then he laughed. I heard more laughter behind me and turned around to see a lobby full of ladies sitting in soft couches and chairs around the outer walls of the lobby. They were all smiling at me through bright red lips. Some were laughing or trying not to laugh.

I must have been a sight for sore eyes with four or five days of Texas road dirt all over me. That was when I decided I was going to find a room with a bath for that night. I started to lift my pack back onto my shoulders and a couple of the ladies came over to help. They smiled at me and squeezed my biceps and forearms tenderly, winked at me and then laughed at each other as they returned to their padded chairs next to the wall. I walked out the door and back into the dirty street.

It really surprised me how much heavier my pack had gotten with people laughing at me. I sure was a sorry sight as I trudged down that dirty street, dodging an occasional mud puddle, and trailing a pack of barking dogs.

I entered an area full of darkies. The men stood in groups of five or six on both sides of the street. Some sat on overturned buckets playing cards, or shooting dice against the wall of a building. Most had a bottle of beer or a jar of moonshine either in their hands or sitting nearby. I passed by some groups of three or four that were singing together in beautiful harmony. From the inside of some buildings came the sound of music, heavy bass sounds with a stead, solid beat. Everyone was happy and smiling and waving to me as I walked by. They laughed and pointed. Fat ladies sat in doorways and yelled at young children playing in the street, and wiped their sweating brows with colorful bandannas. Occasionally, a car, or donkey drawn cart would amble by, and I would stick out my thumb but the passengers would only laugh and wave as they passed me by. A happier group of people, I don't think I had seen anywhere.

The smell reminded me of the barnyard at home. Chickens, dogs, cats, goats, donkeys, and people of all colors, sizes, and shapes were all talking, barking, singing, and yelling at the same time. This was America's melting pot I had heard about in school. With my three or four days of road dirt, I felt like a part of this interesting mixture.

I decided to take one of the side streets to see if I could get away from all the party goers and make better time. I found that the alleys were almost deserted except for an occasional couple locked up tight against each other next to a wall or trashcan. I made good time for the next two or three miles and finally came to a clean looking hotel on a quiet back street. I had to pay two dollars for a room with a bath but it was worth it. I didn't feel safe leaving my stuff in a room if I had to go to the end of the hall for a bath. So, I was glad to have a room with my own bath. I made good use of it too. After I got the road dirt off myself I threw all my clothes in the tub and washed them too.

Two dollars was a lot to spend for a room, but after walking through miles of slums, Mexicans, darkeys, and dogs; I wanted a safe place to bed down and wash up. The newspaper at the hotel said Al Capone had been arrested in Chicago for breaking prohibition laws. He had been in the news a lot lately and the cops were glad to finally get him.

Saturday, June 13, 1931

I caught a ride to Reinhard Bippert's place. Very surprised to see me. Fished in the Medina River. Saw lots of Mexicans. Some were swimming in the river. Lots of new trees and plants.

I caught several rides out to Reinhard Bippert's place. The road was really hot and dusty for my hiking and I stopped at one little Mexican store along the way where I was able to get a 32 oz. Soft drink of lemon lime flavor for only 5 cents. It helped ease the pain of spending $2 for the hotel room.

It seemed to me that half the population in these parts was Mexican. They were very poor and lived in old tumble down shacks next to the road. Most of the shacks had advertisements painted on them and served as signboards. There were no wells and most of them used the river for their water needs. Most of them did day labor in the fields.

Reinhard Bippert was a pen pal I had been corresponding with for five years.

In some farm magazine I had run across the name, Paula Bippert, who wanted a pen pal. Thinking that Paula was a boy's name I answered, and when she wrote back, she said Paula was a girl's name but she had a brother, Reinhard, who was interested in having pen pals. We wrote back and forth for several years but when I wandered into their farm and told them who I was, they were more than surprised, and they sure made me welcome. His mother made us all some chocolate milk, which I drank a lot of in the next couple of days.

The Bippert place was a 200 acre ranch. They raised Longhorn and Brahama cattle in their pasture which appeared to me to be mostly brush. In their fields they raised irrigated corn, oats and milo. Their old farm buildings were nestled in with a variety of large trees: cypress, cottonwood and cedar. The cedar was used for posts which would not only last forever but were needed in their corrals which were 8 to 10 feet tall to control the longhorns and brahamas cattle.

Reinhard took me fishing and swimming on the Medina River. There were many different kinds of trees and plants along our walk. Cactus of a hundred different varieties and lots of Cypress trees with Spanish moss hanging in their branches. When we got to the river there was a group of Mexican boys there with a burro, and a two-wheel cart they were using to get water. They had a wooden stave barrel in the cart and would drive the burro and cart into the river, wait a few minutes for the stream to clear up, and then use pans and pots of various sizes to scoop water into the barrel. When the barrel was as full as the burro could pull out of the stream, they would start yelling at, kicking, pushing and slapping the burro until they would drive him out of the stream, up onto the road and home. They all jabbered in Spanish and all seemed to be talking at once. I couldn't understand a thing they said and wondered if I was still in the United States.

Sunday, June 14, 1931

Fished in the morning. Got nothing. Went to a ball game with Reinhard. Saw part of a Mexican ball game. Very noisy. Took pictures. Lots of cactus around here also Cyprus trees with moss on.

Monday, June 15, 1931

Went to San Antonio and spent the day with his folks. Saw Alamo, museum, park, Market Place Square where Mexicans were. Alamo mission is old, rock fort. Saw room where Bowie was sick in, where the Negro woman hid in.

Visiting the old Alamo made for a very historic day for me. When my grandfather came over from Germany he joined the U.S. Army and fought in the war against Mexico. He helped avenge the massacre that took place at the Alamo years before.

The Bippert family had a Model T Ford and we drove into the city. The market place was filled with Mexicans, darkeys, and whites all trying to sell everything, including goats, pottery, fruits, vegetables, clothes, chickens, you name it, and somebody had it for sale. Everyone advertised by voice, and at the same time, so it was very noisy, dirty and hot. The stench was unbearable. The old Alamo mission and fort is now a museum and park. I visited the room where Jim Bowie, famous for the Bowie knife, was sick and was hidden by a Negro woman. General Sam Houston and 148 Texans were killed here in 1848, including the famous Davy Crockett.

We returned home in time to listen to the *Lum and Abner Show* on the radio and have some more of Mrs. Reinhard's chocolate milk.

Tuesday, June 16, 1931

In the morning Reinhard took me to an irrigation section. I saw canals and locks for the fields. Went to Hondo in the afternoon. Hunted jack rabbits in the evening. Killed some prairie snakes.

In the morning Reinhard drove me out to the Medina River valley irrigation area. It was the first time I had seen how land could be farmed by irrigation. I saw many canals that had locks built along them that could be opened to irrigate the fields whenever the water was needed. It has turned this otherwise very dry area into a very productive area. We drove on over to Hondo, Texas and spent the day there. On the way home it got to be evening and the jackrabbits started to come out into the fields and along the roads. They were plentiful and did a lot of damage to the crops. As we drove along the back roads we could lay over the front fender with Reinhard's 22 rifle and shoot.

I told Reinhard about my experience in Minnesota where I tried to shoot a rabbit with a revolver and how we had planned on having rabbit for supper that night.

"Only Mexicans eat rabbits." He said, wrinkling his forehead and giving me a disgusted look.

We came upon a couple of prairie snakes and killed them too. I didn't even think about suggesting we eat those.

Wednesday, June 17, 1931

Went to an irrigation dam at Medina Lake. Had a big dam to hold water. Over 100 feet deep and thirty miles long. Had small dams to raise water to canal level. Canals ran along hills down to the valley. Fished.

The Medina Dam was built in 1911-1912 by mostly Mexican labor that was paid $2 a day, top wages for that time. The concrete and limestone dam is 164 feet high, 128 feet thick at the base, 25 feet thick at the top, and 1580 feet long. It supplies water to Diversion Lake downstream from which discharges are made to the canal system to irrigate up to 34,000 acres of vegetables, fruit trees, corn, cotton and other crops. Medina Lake, formed by the dam, is 30 miles long and up to 3 miles wide at the widest point, creating 110 miles of shoreline and covers about 5,575 acres.

We found the Medina Lake area was a great place to fish. We still didn't catch anything but it sure was interesting to see how they could trap the river water and then release it down the canals when they wanted to. The canals ran down to a valley where there were lots of fruit farms and we were able to pick our hats full of peaches for 10 cents.

Thursday, June 18, 1931

Packed up to leave tomorrow. Heard from home. Hank Lampman said Ralph Garthwait and Miss Quarnie were married. Heard that Milton Ellis had drowned. Swam with sixteen Mexicans in the Medina River.

Friday, June 19, 1931

Bipperts took me to San Antonio. Caught ride in an old Ford into Houston. We pulled into the city at two o'clock at night. Bunked aside the road on edge of town.

The Bipperts left me off on the edge of town on my road to Houston. Rides were really hard to come by again and I had to do a lot of walking. The road was dusty and hot but one ride I got I've always remembered. I was sitting by the side of the road waiting for a ride to show up when an old darkey came along with a pair of mules hitched to an old wagon. The wagon had three seats. The back two were just hand sawed boards laid across the sides of the wagon. There were five or six darkey kids holding these seats down. The old darkey man sat up front by himself, stopped the mules and said. "You want a ride?"

"I'd be more than happy to ride awhile. It would sure beat this standing and walking in this hot sun." I replied and climbed up on the seat next to him. The darkey kids kept their eyes on me, and didn't say much during our ride.

"Where you from?" He asked.

"Wisconsin."

"Is that in these here United States?"

"Yes sir, it's a long way north of here where it gets real cold in the winter time."

"Don't sound like no place I'd wanna be."

"Well, where you from?" I asked in return.

"Up this here road a piece, and then over that a ways a little." Was his reply, as he pointed to the right with his left hand.

"I done lived there all my life."

"Who owns all these houses in the cotton fields?" I asked.

"Well, most of them are owned by whatever white man owns the cotton field. He builds them for his workers. They work the land for a share of the crops and live in those shacks. Ain't what I would call a house. They can plant their own garden and have some chickens or livestock if they want to. Some even owns his own house, but not very many. Most of us just work for the man."

I rode for more than an hour with them until they turned off the road.

My next ride was in an old Ford that got me into Houston around two o'clock at night. I bunked aside the road on the edge of town.

Saturday, June 20, 1931

Went through Houston. Caught a ride to Galveston. Looked the shipping yards over and beach over. Fished in the gulf. Went back to Houston. Caught ride to Beaumont. A half-drunk man showed me where to sleep.

It was in Houston that I began to notice that the whites and darkeys do business together but they are socially separated into two separate classes. I saw divided seating in streetcars, different restaurants, theaters, drinking fountains, restrooms, and most any other place you can think of. It was something I had never seen before and I can't say I agreed with it or saw any reason for it at all. But it was the way they chose to live or were forced to live, I didn't know which, but it sure was different from Wisconsin.

I got one ride early in the morning and got into Galveston. It was an interesting city, more so because it is on the gulf and the harbor was full of ships from all over the world. When I saw all the ships I thought maybe I could get a ride on one and work my way over to the East Coast. I walked all along the harbor from one ship to another. It was quite a sight to see. The sailors, from all nations, were tough looking, dark skinned, most of them with no shirt, just old pants and shoes. They were unshaven, had scars or tattoos somewhere on their bodies, and most had teeth missing. Some were loading, and some were unloading merchandise of all kinds. I saw cotton, sulfur, and oil. Just to mention a few. One old cook was peeling potatoes by the water so he had a place to throw the peels. I could not understand any of the languages they spoke. After seeing such a dirty crew I wanted no part in asking anyone for a trip on a boat to the East Coast.

I had fish line with me and after getting some squid for bait I sat out on one pier for an hour or more and fished. I got one sand shark about a foot long. The men fishing next to me caught lots of strange looking fish that I didn't know their names. Early in the afternoon I had enough of Galveston so I got back on the highway to Houston. A happy half-drunk man showed me a park where there were plenty of trees and a good place to make camp for the night.

Sunday, June 21, 1931

Caught short rides to Oberlin, Louisiana. Took train to Oakdale, because of detour. Caught a long ride through Alexandria to Standard. Slept in a cutover forest. Lots of lumber mills around here.

This was a very interesting day for me. The man that picked me up in Oakdale and gave me the long ride asked me if I had ever heard of Evangeline and Gabriel from Longfellow's poem. I told him I had, and he went on to say that his forefathers were among the Frenchmen chased out of Nova Scotia around 1755. Over 2500 of these exiles were driven south, looking for some place to live. They drifted down the coast and finally settled along the bayous in central Louisiana. His grandmother still lived back in the bayou and he was going in to visit her on his way through, and if I wanted to go along I was welcome.

We left the main road somewhere and kept taking side roads, then side roads that were more trails than roads. We went through one swamp after another, always following the high ground around swamps and streams. We came to his Grandmother's home. It was built on stilts, beside a small river, with a few open patches of ground and the rest large trees close to the river.

It was an old, unpainted house, built from home-sawed lumber and with a tin roof, there were no screens on the door or windows, dogs and chickens wandered aimlessly around the yard. His Grandmother was sure glad to see us, and the first thing she did was set up a table with squash, corn, potatoes, beans, some kind of fish, and what looked to be chicken and rice, but could have been some other kind of bird.

"My, this sure is a pile of food for us to lunch on." I said.

"Honey, we Cajuns don't eat to live. We live to eat." She replied with a big smile spreading across her face.

She was a very old lady, went barefoot but her clothes were really clean. She said she had relatives in the area, but none that I met.

These French Arcadians were now known as the Cajuns of the swamp country in Louisiana. They took up fishing, trapping, hunting, and some small farming and logging in the bayous. That has been their way of life for years but a few, like my friend the driver, had gotten to the outside and were losing the Cajun way of life.

Monday, June 22, 1931

Got short rides to Monroe, LA. Took a bus into Monroe. Picked up and taken to Clarksdale, Mississippi. They gave me supper, bed, and bath. His address is John N. Peterson, 739 Desota St., Clarksdale. Poor roads in Mississippi and lots of darkeys.

After taking a bus to the outskirts of Monroe I was picked up by Mr and Mrs. Peterson who had a five or six year old son along. They had been traveling and were on their way home. Their son was restless and when I got in the back seat of the car, from then on, all day long, it was my job to play games, read and tell stories to the young lad. This really pleased the parents and I traveled all day with them. They even talked it over in the afternoon how I could spend the night with them, which was certainly okay with me.

We crossed the Mississippi River on a ferry. The state of Mississippi had terrible roads. They were gravel, dusty and rough. Mr. Peterson was kept really busy dealing with deep ruts, potholes, and generally roads that showed no upkeep or maintenance. There were lots of darkeys walking along the roads and working the fields. Many still used mules or horses in the fields. They were using oxen to haul logs out of the woods. Most of the farmers were really poor in this area and it made me realize that I really had not seen or appreciated how much I had until I was able to see and experience how much others didn't have.

We were all ready for a good bath when we got to their home in Clarksburg. I was treated royally for taking care of the young lad and they gave me a big supper, a nice hot bath, and a soft bed. A big breakfast the next day too.

I learned by reading the Peterson's paper that evening that President Hoover had proposed that all war debts should be suspended for a year to help revitalize world trade. Mr. Peterson thought that would make it easier for them to sell their cotton crop to the countries overseas. He was really excited.

Tuesday, June 23, 1931

Had my breakfast. Caught a ride into Memphis, Tenn. Had to walk for three hours through the city. Caught an 80-mile ride with old car. through heavy rain. Slept in an old haystack

During my walk through Memphis I passed by the harbor on the Mississippi River and thought I might get a ride up river with one of the many barges or paddle wheelers working the river.

As I was asking about work, a man offered me a ride in an old Model T that still had the old brass headlights that burned coal oil. It didn't look like we would be able to make it another mile in the old thing, but by evening, when he left me off, we had gone 80 miles.

I was out in the country. It had rained heavy at times and just before dark I saw what I thought was a haystack close to the road. I went over and dug in, unwrapped my canvas, and thought I had a good place for the night. In a couple of hours I couldn't stand the smell anymore. What I thought was a haystack turned out to be an old rotten sorghum pile. It was dark and lightening some but I packed up and got back on the road to look for some other camping area.

I walked quite a ways using the lightening for light, and before long I saw an old shack fairly close to the road. From the light of the lightening it surely looked deserted. I thought I had it made for sure until I went down and opened the door and heard a darkey say something to his wife. What he said I don't know but I closed the door as gently as I could and got back on the highway. I was scared the old fellow might have a shotgun and would be wondering who opened his door at that time of night. If I would have stayed in the yard and called out to announce my arrival, he might have let me sleep on the floor but I was too shook up by his being there that I quickly headed on down the road in the dark, with only the lightning to light my way.

Down the road a ways, I spotted a good haystack, dug in for the rest of the night, and the next morning I washed up good in a stream to get some of the stink off me.

Wednesday, June 24, 1931

Caught a ride with four merry makers. They were half drunk and had plenty with them. Went through Kentucky, crossed on a ferry and went into Missouri, then crossed bridge back to Cairo, Illinois. Slept on other side of Carbondale.

The weather was hot and muggy. I had washed my clothes and put them on wet and they dried out as I walked. Two young men and two ladies picked me up and what they were celebrating I don't know but they talked a lot, drank a lot and drove very fast. Fact is, I was glad when they left me off, but I made a good many miles with them. I thought I would go up to Chicago and then east but my best way was to go over into Missouri and then get to Cairo, Ill. Hitching rides was easy and by night I was well up in Illinois.

Thursday, June 25, 1931

Caught rides and rode into Chicago with a man. Hunted up Ed Holley. Jessie was in Wisconsin. Stayed with Mr. Holley all night. Very warm, very smoky around there. They have a nice home.

As I was approaching Chicago it looked like a big, black storm was coming up. I found out later it was air pollution. Jessie was my first cousin. Ed was surprised when I walked in. Their home is in Berwgn, not too far from downtown Chicago. Ed fed me everything he could. Had the use of a hot bathtub, which was very welcome. We listened to *The Amos 'n' Andy Show* on the radio that evening.

Friday, June 26, 1931

Walked a ways from Chicago. Caught rides. About six o'clock, a college student on his way to New Jersey, picked me up. Has an old Ford. We went a ways and slept just over the boundary in Ohio.

The young man was Milo Pitcher from Collins, Iowa. He was four years older than I was and about a foot taller. He had the old Ford and we had a wonderful time for the next five days traveling east. I bought some gas every so often. We often fixed our own meals, changed off driving and the old Model T purred right along. No top on the car so we had plenty of wind and sun.

Saturday, June 27, 1931

Went through Ohio with him. Went through Pittsburgh, Pennsylvania, crossed West Virginia and Ohio Rivers. Slept 53 miles east of Pittsburgh. He took a room and I slept by the car. Very hilly country around Pittsburgh.

After traveling through Ohio we came to the city of Pittsburgh, Pennsylvania. It was a city filled with huge iron foundries and big hills. On one hillside we could look down and see three streets below us. We were also able to look right inside the foundries and see the huge white-hot iron bars being cooled.

The old Model T had quite a time with the hills too. Many times it needed a running start to climb the hills. More than once we would run out of gas because the gas was gravity fed from the tank under the front seat to the motor. We would turn around and using the reverse pedal, which had a lower gear ratio, we were able to climb even the steepest hill because the gas would then be higher than the motor.

I was the official watchman at night. We would find a place to park, usually in a grove of trees and I would bed down for the night near the car and Milo would take a room. I had the cooking utensils and often we cooked up egg sandwiches and opened a can of beans and had a good meal.

Sunday, June 28, 1931

Crossed Allegheny and Blue Ridge Mountains. Went over old battlefields. Got to Washington D.C. Went around Capitol, Washington Monument, White House and saw the city. Had a hard time to find a place to sleep. Very beautiful place.

Monday, June 29, 1931

Went through Mt. Vernon, Capitol, Washington Monument. Walked down it, 900 steps, 555 feet tall. On White House grounds, looked in windows. Went through Baltimore. Camped ten miles from Delaware.

By the time we got to Washington D.C. the old Model T had no brakes and many rattles. We had the worst looking car in D.C. When we would stop at a stop sign, steam would roll out of the radiator and everyone would stop, look and listen to our old Tin Lizzie. In these days it was easy to get around. Not much traffic, streetcars ran all through the city. Horse drawn wagons were on all the roads delivering ice, freight and whatever had to be moved.

We never worried about parking the Ford with our gear in it, unlocked, and going in all these historic places.

Milo had time before taking a job for the summer in New Jersey. We did all of the sightseeing we could. We took an elevator to the top of the Washington Monument and we decided to walk down. 900 steps were quite a walk and our legs felt like rubber when we finally got on the ground. At the Capitol we hired a guide to show us the Senate and Representative Chambers. At the White House we were too late to get in on the tour, so we looked in the windows into the Blue Room. The lawns around the White House were kept beautiful.

We drove through Arlington Cemetery and saw the Tomb of the Unknown Soldier and the changing of the guards, which was very impressive. Then we drove 13 miles down the Potomac River to Mt. Vernon. It cost us twenty-five cents to enter and was all like it was when George Washington lived there. We walked down to the river to see the boathouse and pier that were in badly decayed condition.

Drove on through Baltimore and made camp 10 miles from Delaware.

Tuesday, June 30, 1931

Went through Philadelphia, Delaware and started hiking from Trenton, New Jersey. Went through New York City. Saw the skyline, Statue of Liberty, Empire Building, 1250 feet tall, Woolworth Building, etc.

Rode in a subway 10 miles through the city. Got a ride with Senator Yates of New Jersey. Camped 25 miles north of the city.

This was a big long day for me. Said goodbye to Milo in Trenton and started walking. Senator Yates from New Jersey picked me up in a really nice car. He was a really nice man and asked me where all I had been. He seemed really interested in all my stories. He carried me right up to the edge of New York City. A few years later I saw a piece in the paper about him being shot by his blond girlfriend.

I had quite a time going through New York City. I crossed the Hudson River by ferry and saw the skyline as I approached. I must have had to ask a dozen times which streetcar to take to head north. I ended up once down by the waterfront where I saw lots of really large ships loading and unloading and could see the Statue of Liberty. Walked through some streets downtown and saw many people standing in lines. Some were applying for jobs and some were waiting for food. I saw the Empire State building that is 1250 feet tall but the top was lost in the clouds. I walked by the Woolworth Building and lots of other skyscrapers. One cop finally told me to get on the subway and ride under the city to the north. When I finally got to the edge of the city I picked up some short rides. All the cities are very close together and I couldn't tell when I was leaving one city and entering another. They were filled with factories and many were still using waterpower to drive their machinery. Nearly all the people worked in factories.

I saw a few small, rocky farms and some truck farming in Delaware and New Jersey near the large cities but very few wire fences. All fences were either rails or rocks.

Wednesday, July 1, 1931

Got short rides to Cambridge, Mass. One man nearly ran over a man. Saw where Old Washington Elm stood, Old Church, Longfellow's home. Camped in a public park. Was given directions by a man I rode with.

The East was very historic, most of the places I visited I had read about in school. Cambridge Common was the park I spent the night in. It was a big public park with lots of big trees and some large evergreen trees had branches spread way out and down to the ground. When it got fairly dark I crawled under the branches and found a good place to spread my canvas for the night. I don't think they wanted campers in the park but the way I was hid it woulda taken a hound to find me. Cambridge and Boston were all hooked together with streetcars. So, the next day I spent touring Boston.

Thursday, July 2, 1931

Went through historic places in Boston. The old State House, Fennel Hall, Old North Church, Paul Revere's Home, Bunker Hill. Went through Harvard Museum. Visited the Navy yard. The Old

Constitution left the yard a half-hour before I got there. Got rides to Portland, Maine. Slept in a hay field.

It was a busy day. I didn't spend too much time in any one place and a lot of places were fairly close together so I was able to see a lot in a short time. The streets in downtown were narrow and crooked. I saw the Old State House that was built in 1657 and rebuilt in 1713. It was here they held the first legislature, drew up the constitution, had the Boston Massacre, and whipping post and stocks. Next was the Old North Church where Paul Revere was signaled. They still hold services there every Sunday. Paul Revere's Home was nearby and a group of dirty children were curious about my packsack and me and started following me around. I saw the Harvard Museum and Bunker Hill where I had to pay ten cents to climb to the top of the monument which gave me a really good view of the old city and the harbor. But my sore feet and heavy pack kept me from doing much charging up that hill. I went on down to the Navy yard and found out the Old Constitution ship had left just a half an hour before I got there.

The fish market surrounded Fennel Hall and I could smell it before I got to it. They displayed their fish, crabs and lobsters in tubs of ice right out in the street. Horse drawn carts delivering everything, including the flies that follow horses, were in sight all around downtown and by the waterfront. It was hot and foul smelling and the dirtiest place I have ever been in my life. Most of the people were foreigners who lived in the apartments nearby. There were dirty children playing cards, dice, or with little sail boats in the dirty water puddles.

I was glad to get out of town and was lucky getting rides to Portland, Maine. I was on a gravel and dirt road looking for a place to camp and I saw this good hay field. The hay was probably three feet tall, so I got off the road, out in the field a ways and bedded down for the night.

Friday, July 3, 1931

Woke up and a man was trying to set a big police dog on me. Got out in a hurry. One man gave me a dollar. Tried to get a job with a carnival in Lancaster, New Hampshire. Camped by the Connecticut River in the White Mountains in Vermont.

When I woke up in the morning and stood up I heard a voice and looked over by a home about a block or so away. There was a man trying to show a police dog where I was and sic him on me. I took one look, the dog was jumping around and I didn't know if he spotted me or not. I ducked down in the hay, packed up my packsack and took out my knife, held it in one hand and ran for the road. I was sure mad at that man but the dog never came after me. I traveled along the coastline north and the scenery was really beautiful. A little old winding road ran around the bluffs close to the water. The ocean was too rough to get close to the water.

I stopped at a roadside restaurant by the water and went in and ordered a glass of milk and a hamburger. When the cook brought it out he said 35 cents, ten cents for the milk and twenty-five cents for the burger. I backed up a bit and said I would never pay that much for milk and a burger. That the most I had been paying was 5 cents for milk and either 10 cents or 15 cents for a burger. That made the cook mad and he jerked the stuff off the counter, swore at me and said to get the hell out of there. I wasn't in too good a mood anyway; first thing have a dog set on me then having this man trying to overcharge me. I picked up my pack and walked on up the road.

Later on a man gave me a ride and I was telling him about my morning experiences and he got such a bang out of it he gave me a dollar when he left me off. He said it was worth a dollar to hear my story.

A carnival was playing in Lancaster and I thought it might be fun to work in one for a while. I looked up the manager in a trailer house and he said no, all filled up. I crossed over into Vermont and made camp by the Connecticut River, in foothills of the White Mountains.

Saturday, July 4, 1931

Crossed the Green Mountains in Vermont. Went by Lake Chaplain. Rode on a motorcycle into Canada. Lots of drunk Americans in Canada. Got to Montreal. Took a hotel. Saw two of Al Capone's restaurants. Lots of holdups.

Ride getting was easy in 1931. The eastern states were small and often I traveled in two states the same day. I was by Lake Champaign enjoying all the beautiful scenery and the large hotels around there. I was told it cost $80 and up to stay one night. I figured I wouldn't be able to afford to stay even one minute. A man on a motorcycle stopped. He was headed for Canada and said I could ride on the back seat. With my pack on my back we headed north. It was the only motorcycle ride I had hitchhiking and it was a good one. We had no trouble crossing the boundary. I told them I had an uncle in Ottawa and was going to visit. Mostly all French language used around Montreal. I had a really hard time making people understand what I wanted. Got a cheap hotel and cleaned up.

Sunday, July 5, 1931

Caught short rides to Ottawa. Lots of French going to picnics in trucks. Young boys taking girls out riding in horse and buggy. Found Uncle Hamp Allen's place. Gone fishing. One girl home. Left pack and came back when they were home.

I had a hard time catching rides between Montreal and Ottawa. There were very few cars. I did see a lot of fast road horses or ponies. The young couples were out in horse and buggies and the men would drive with one hand when they were with their lady friends. When Uncle Hamp and Aunt Margarett and the rest of the girls came back from fishing and saw my packsack they hardly knew what to expect. They had come back to Wisconsin when I was five years old and brought Glen, Rud and me each a deerskin book or school bag. That was about all I could remember of them, the book bags they brought us. I soon found myself surrounded by five girls and their parents. They surely made me welcome.

Monday, July 6, 1931

Got up late. Very good meals. Ate lots. Wrote letters. Went swimming in the river with the girls. Five girls are home: Olga, Eva, Ruth, Famine and Retta. Have a nice home in the country and a large garden.

Tuesday, July 7, 1931

Wrote letters in the forenoon, went swimming again. Uncle Hamp drove me around the city in the evening. Beautiful driveways and parks. Saw the capitol buildings. Very pretty, like cathedrals.

Uncle Hamp had an electrical business and said a few years before the Queen of England came over and he got the job of lighting up the capitol buildings.

Wednesday, July 8, 1931

Played golf in the yard. Went to office downtown. Large office, 18 men on the payroll. Went to a show with Famine who is the stenographer. Went on the lake in a rowboat in the evening with Fill and Ruth. Uncle Hamp bought me some lightweight pants and tennis shoes.

Thursday, July 9, 1931

Played tennis all afternoon. Went swimming in the evening. About eleven o'clock we got word that someone was in Uncle's office. Thought it was robbers, called police, went down, it was just friends.

Friday, July 10, 1931

Helped Retta pull weeds. Went with Olga through a museum. A funny gink tried to follow us there. Went to a show. Betty Light is over most of the time. Made candy.

Saturday, July 11, 1931

The Orangemen had their picnic. They're a rough sort of lodge. The regatta boat races were held. In the evening went with Famine, Betty, and Olga to Lake Chateau. Two strangers offered us a lift in their car.

Sunday, July 12, 1931

Got up early and went to White Lake fishing. Retta, Eva, Uncle Hamp and I went. We got four bass. Beautiful place. Picked some blueberries. Got home at ten. They want me to stay until August 1st.

Monday, July 13, 1931

Rained all day. Went swimming. Went for a ride in the evening with Famine and her boy friend, Michael Keogan, and Mary Faucet. Went up in Laurencha Mountains then back. Got in at 12 o'clock. Nice kids.

Tuesday, July 14, 1931

Went around with Uncle Hamp. Up to some millionaire folks. In evening went with Famine to a vaudeville show. Good show. Got passes for it. Was in a slaughterhouse today.

Wednesday, July 15, 1931

Got up at 9 o'clock and played tennis then read books. In evening went for a ride with Famine and Michel. Picked up another girl in the telephone office. I drove the car home.

Thursday, July 16, 1931

Helped pick berries. In the afternoon Famine and I went through Parliament buildings. Saw a 20-ton bell that was in the Peace

Tower. Listened to Parliament setting. Very beautiful buildings with a large library. Spies in the war burned the place.

We had seats in the balcony and listened to the Parliament in session. One thing they discussed in length was about sending hay way north to feed the reindeer. How much to send, the cost and where to send it. It seemed the reindeer were running out of feed and hay was needed.

Friday, July 17, 1931

Read books most of the day. Ruth and Fill went to visit in Montreal. Ruth bought a Persian rug that was smuggled in. The Ottawa River is filled with logs for paper pulp.

Saturday, July 18, 1931

Read books. Went swimming with Famine. Kay Grant was over again. She and Betty filled my pajamas with safety pins. Over to Betty's a while played cards. Had good lunch.

Sunday, July 19, 1931

Went for a drive in the afternoon to Clayton Lake. Lots of pines, rock and berries. Mostly rail fences. Michel K. was up in evening. Has a lot of fun. Intend to leave in another week.

Monday, July 20, 1931

Rained today. Got a letter from home. Heard that Glen and Clark Abram had to leave their boat in Kentucky and start hitchhiking to New Mexico. Went swimming at 10 o'clock at night.

Glen and Clark had the idea of taking a big row boat and floating down the Mississippi River to New Orleans then go west from there. The river got too big and wild down south, too hard a going for them, so they sold the boat and headed west on foot.

Tuesday, July 21, 1931

Fermine, Mary Faucet, Michael and I went through a paper mill. Saw them grind pulp and make paper. Had a picnic supper in the hills. Went to Lunac Park afterwards. Rode on the Sky-chaser, Whip and etc.

Wednesday, July 22, 1931

Slept late. Fixed a screen for Aunt Margaret. Went swimming. Famine tried to show me how to dance. Went swimming again in the evening.

Thursday, July 23, 1931

Read and tinkered around in the forenoon. Ritta and I went to a show in the afternoon. All vaudeville. Met some of Aunt

Margarett's cousins in the evening. Mrs. Light fainted and fell. She was bruised up.

Friday, July 24, 1931

Couldn't get into the mint. Went to a show in the afternoon with Famine. At night went to a wrestling match with Jim and Uncle Hemp. Muloney, 6 feet and 7 inches tall lost to Gus Sonnenburg. Gus used his flying tackle; he is the world champion.

Saturday, July 25, 1931

Olga and Betty went to Toronto. I went through the mint and saw them making 50 cent pieces. Held a gold brick that was worth $12,000. Went through the archives, high school. Down to dance hall at night.

Sunday, July 26, 1931

Hit the road again. Uncle Hamp took me to the St. Lawrence River at Ogdensburg. Crossed on a ferry. The officers didn't want to let me back in the USA. Got short rides. Slept in park at Syracuse, New York.

Monday, July 27, 1931

Woke up and saw a sign saying $10 fine for trespassing, so I pulled up and left. Saw the state prison at Auburn. Through

Geneva at Senaca Lake. Got to Niagara Falls. Slept in a tourist camp for 25 cents. The falls are very beautiful. There are two sides with an island in the middle. The falls are about 125 feet tall with colored lights illuminating them at night.

Tuesday, July 28, 1931

Left Niagara Falls. Got short rides to Buffalo. Walked about eight miles through Buffalo. Followed the lake to Buffalo. Beautiful drive. Went through Erie, Pennsylvania. Rode with a couple. Got to Cleveland, Ohio. Found Uncle Frank Allen's home in an apartment house. Got there about 8:30 and he was very glad to see me. Feet are sore.

Wednesday, July 29, 931

Stayed at Uncle Frank's place. We walked down town and went to a show in the afternoon. Uncle Frank works in a blue print office. Washed my clothes. When traveling I wash them in creeks.

Thursday, July 30, 1931

Left Cleveland. Got short rides for 80 miles. A Wisconsin boy traveling from Maine picked me up on way to Wisconsin. Got to within 25 miles of South Bend, Indiana. Had car trouble. Slept in a park. Saw President Hayes' home in Fremont.

Friday, July 31, 1931

Got car fixed. Went through Chicago. Left note on Ed Holley's door. Left the Maine boy in Whitewater. Got to Madison. Found Professor Lampman at tent colony.

Went swimming.

Saturday, August 1, 1931

Went swimming four times today. Met Hank's friends. Had a good rain. They have a nice camp in a tent in a large tent colony by the lake.

Sunday, August 2, 1931

Went swimming several times. Went to a show in the afternoon. In the evening his friends and I went for a walk up to Black Hawk Cave where he once hid.

Monday, August 3, 1931

Bought books. The Lampman family took me out of town on the road toward home. Got short rides home. Arrived at 9 o'clock. Everyone in bed. Just got through thrashing at home.

That ended my summer hitchhiking trip. When I left home I had $50 on me and when I got back I had $13 left. I had covered 37 states at an average cost of $1 per state, besides being in Canada. Now I was ready to go back and finish my senior year of high school.

Al Kussmaul

A YEAR ON THE BUM

Allen Kussmaul

I was going to the Madison Business College called the 4C School. I got a letter from my brother Glen   saying he wanted to head west early in the spring. He wasn't in the best of health, asthma bothered him quite a bit in the damp Wisconsin climate, and he also was bothered with epileptic seizures ever so often. He didn't like to travel alone and asked if I would go with him. He wanted to get in a dryer climate where he could breathe better and the asthma wouldn't bother him so much.

I was game to go. It was early in the spring when he wrote me so I finished up my school work a month ahead of schedule, got passing grades, and headed for home.

We spent a few days getting our gear together. We had quite a list but we had to keep it down so it would all fit in our pack sacks. We each had a good heavy canvas packsack with two shoulder straps so it fit on our backs in good shape, good sturdy leather shoes, a new hat, one extra shirt, an extra pair of pants, a 6 foot by 5 foot light canvas, small frying pan, two 8 foot poles, a canteen, tin plate, good pocket knife, fork and spoons. For grub to start with, we had oatmeal, raisins, cocoa, bacon, a loaf of homemade bread, salt and pepper, rice and numerous other small items.

Our packs were full, probably weighed 35 to 40 pounds each. We adjusted the shoulder straps so the pack fit high and square on our backs, it had to fit just right so our arms would hang free. We each had a money belt, about three inches wide that we wore under our shirts with about thirty dollars; most of it was kept in the money belts, the rest in the old fashioned snap pocket books.

May 7, 1933, from my log book.

"Glen and I left home today on what is to be a merry old bum through the west. Rud took us to Prairie du Chien where we walked across the bridge and started for Dubuque, Iowa. A fellow by the name of Blane Ashton picked us up and we went west 250 miles to Spencer, Iowa.

We had planned on going south to Dubuque but when we were offered such a good long ride west, we couldn't refuse.

It rained hard all afternoon and we were lucky because we didn't have any rain coats. Ashton is a friend of Babe Ruth. We put up in a tourist cabin for one dollar. I had dreams all night and kept Glen awake."

May 8, 1933

"We got up at eight o'clock and hit Highway 71 straight south, headed for Kansas City, Missouri or Dallas, Texas. We intend to get into a warmer climate before we go west. I started getting sandwiches from farmers. I always ask to buy a couple and they usually gave them to me. At night we found a nice small straw stack and we made camp in it. We haven't any blankets so we tore off a lot of straw and burrowed in like hogs. We were about 180 miles south of Spencer."

May 9, 1933

"We woke up last night and a big storm was coming up, so we tore off the top of the straw pile and we crawled under about two or three feet of straw to finish the night. It didn't rain much but the straw pile squashed us. The mice chewed Glen's hat up and made it look like the devil. I couldn't see straight and when I looked at my watch I thought it was half past six so we got up and then found it was only a little after five. I took a picture of Glen when he had his head sticking out of the straw.

We started to bum breakfast; we came to two farms right across the road from one another. Glen went to one and I went to the other. We both asked for sandwiches for both of us and said the other fellow went to the other farm house for water. I guess the lady where Glen went caught on to our trick because she charged Glen thirty cents for two and I got four for nothing. Glen was laughing all the time on her porch and he couldn't look at her with a straight face because of what we were doing. Went on a detour to Bedford and I'm bumming grub and saving it up. I made one blunder by getting two egg sandwiches and thanking the lady and started walking away before I happened to remember that I had offered to buy them.

A truck came along and could only haul one of us, so Glen went to St. Joseph with it. I got there and met him at night. He thought he saw a good straw pile to sleep in, so we headed out of the city. It was dark and after crossing an onion field our noses told us that we had come to the city manure pile instead of a straw pile. We tried to find another but couldn't. We tried sleeping in a dairy delivery horse wagon but froze out in a few minutes. We walked till one o'clock and found ourselves in another end of St. Joseph. We lay on a park bench but the cops flashed their lights on us. Then we got in a box car but froze out so we started walking to keep warm for the rest of the night."

When traveling the way we did, we usually had time on our hands while walking. When no rides were in sight and as we passed by good looking farms, we would bum sandwiches and save them up. Usually by the end of the day our packs were full of good things to eat. Some ladies would throw in some cookies, donuts or even cake. When we split up we had a system to know where to meet in the next city. We kept certain gum wrappers and we left a note in the wrapper and the first one into town would go to the post office and leave the wrapper on the right hand side of the main steps going in. There is usually some trash lying around so our wrapper never looked out of place. We used this system several times and it worked perfectly. I have seen several people watch me picking through the trash, picking up a wrapper and reading a note that was tucked inside.

May 10, 1933, Wednesday.

"About 5 o'clock a truck picked us up and carried us to Kansas City, we looked the city over and went down to the stockyards. We had to walk out of the city and we couldn't catch a ride, so we agreed to split up and meet at El Paso, Texas next Tuesday; giving us six days to make it in. I caught a hundred mile ride and saw Glen pass by in a faster car. I got to Pittsburg, Kansas. I was going to sleep by a river but I saw a storm coming up, so I went back to Pittsburg. There were no box cars empty and when I found a large mortar box, I crawled under that. I slept for perhaps twenty minutes when the storm hit. I found myself nearly floating in water. I got out of there and got in a lumber yard. I was too cold and wet to sleep and at three o'clock I started walking the highway."

I remember that morning well because when it got daylight I could look myself over. My clothes were covered from head to foot with mud; some still wet, some just glued or caked to my clothes. I was a mess from head to foot. The lumber yard where I crawled in was covered with thick dust; all roads back then were either dirt or thin gravel and what blew in the lumber yard stayed there. Later in the morning I was still walking and close to the road was a nice stream. I went over to the stream and in a nice brush place I found a nice big pond of water. I took off all my clothes excepting my shorts, washed my pants, shirt, socks and anything else with mud on it. I only had one other option. While I was busy washing my clothes, along came two ladies with fishing poles, they moved on downstream. I washed everything, rung it

78

out good and put it on wet. That system worked well, my clothes soon dried out in the dry, southern air.

May 11, 1933.

"I walked all morning to keep warm and after a few short rides I got to Picture 1, Oklahoma. It's a mining town. The country is covered with old lead and zinc mines. Five fellows held up a place where cars are transferred from the railroad to the truckers. They shot and killed one fellow. I got short rides all forenoon and then a truck driver, who was pulling three Fords, picked me up. I rode all the way to the Texas line in his truck. He got awfully sleepy and several times I had to nudge him or he would have run off the road. We bought a steak for supper. The biggest I ever saw and only 25 cents. It was fully sixteen inches by ten inches and was all I could eat. We got to the car station on the border and I helped him unload and about three o'clock we got in a new Ford eight and started for Dallas, Texas. He ran the car right along, and the roads were crooked. All at once he kind of dozed off and the car was going about fifty and we left the road. We just missed a bridge and landed in a ditch but we didn't hurt anything. I drove the rest of the way into Dallas and we got in at five-thirty in the morning. I left my hat in his car. I got off in a park and got a couple hours sleep."

My ride with this Ford delivery man was one of the longest rides I had without sleep. He was really sleepy from being on the road so long and I had to stay awake, keep talking and once in a while nudge him to keep him awake. When I took over the driving he went sound asleep and I had to drive and fight sleep the rest of the way into Dallas. He told me where he was going and on what street, so after sleeping in the park I hunted up the street and walked all around and thought maybe I could spot the car we drove and get my hat back, but no luck.

May 12, 1933,

"After leaving the park I walked a couple miles back to the edge of town where I found a large, clean stream to wash myself and my clothes in. I took off all my clothes except my shorts and got out in the middle of the stream and started washing myself and my clothes. I heard a car door slam and on looking up I found two young ladies watching me. They were as much surprised as I was. I told them to back off for a minute and then I put on my wet pants and sweater. I went on washing clothes and they came back and started fishing. It was about one o'clock when I got out of Dallas and started walking to Ft. Worth. In about two hours I made the city. I passed through the city and started toward El Paso. That road was expected to be one of the worst hitchhiking roads in the country. Right off the bat I caught a ride with a fellow who had been in a tornado the day before. I travelled seventy miles with him. The country is getting more barren. There are some small plains where cattle graze. Towns are few and far between.

I crawled over a board fence into a football field to spend the night. I found a good windbreak and then after finding some boards to lie on, I went to sleep. I must have been dreaming or else I had a nightmare and started walking in my sleep. All at once, in the middle of the night; I got up, packed my bag, climbed over the board fence and started walking the highway. After walking for perhaps a half mile I gradually came to my senses. I cussed myself and started looking for another place to sleep. I saw a large sign out in a pasture and I went out there and lay down back of it. I slept for about an hour when a bull came bellowing around, so I jumped up and started looking for another place to finish my night's sleep. I found a hedge, which was a good windbreak, and I laid down there for a while. In a couple of hours it started raining so I got up again to find a dry place. Through the lightening I could see a bushy tree out in a field. I got under it and slept for the rest of the night. Early in the morning I had to get up three times and throw stones at a bird that insisted on singing in my tree and keeping me awake."

That was one of the longest nights I had trying to get some rest. After the two days of traveling, I must have been overly tired, besides getting caught twice now with my pants down washing clothes and bathing. In one of the cities I had gone through, I found a second hand store that sold most everything and I bought a Texas style hat. It was too hot in the daytime not to have something on my head. In the south everyone wore large brimmed hats, so I was right in style.

May 13, 1933, Saturday.

"Ride getting was awful tough today. In the forenoon I walked for eight or nine miles at a stretch. I got sick of it and said to hell with hitchhiking. At one o'clock I got to a town by the name of Strawn. I went down to the railroad yards and was determined to get my first freight train ride. A train just pulled in from the east headed toward El Paso. I found myself a good front seat on a tank car and sat there and waited for it to go. A young lad of about eleven or twelve was on the same car. He was heading west just to find a place to stay. I gave him some grub and then we began to wonder when the train would leave. After sitting there for three hours I asked a brakeman when the train would leave. He said the train wasn't going any further, that they would just take it out in pieces. That made me mad and I said, "To hell with the freight trains." And again I hit the highway. I got a short ride to the other side of Abilene. I stopped at a farm house and asked to do some work for a bite to eat. They didn't have any work to do but they gave me two egg sandwiches and a glass of milk. I think I'll try that again some time. I begged some newspapers and went out in a field to put up for the night. About eleven o'clock I froze out and I headed back to town where I had seen an empty box car. One corner of it was filled with paper so I made a warm nest for the rest of the night."

May 14, 1933. Sunday.

"It started raining and it rained all forenoon. I finally got to Sweetwater where I was again going to get a freight train. I walked with a bunch of other bums until three o'clock. A man saw me on a street corner and he gave me a good chicken dinner."

Most every main road city has a place where the bums or hoboes or drifters, whatever you want to call them, hang out. This they call "the jungle". The jungle by Abilene was a large brush patch, mostly willow, cottonwoods, and other trees. There would be campfire places, maybe some pails or cans hanging on limbs of trees, some places even had a frying pan hanging on a nail on a tree. Usually the jungle was by a creek or small stream of some kind where everyone could wash up some, do dishes, or wash clothes. On this particular day being Sunday and this being one of my first days when I was determined to get on a freight train, I went down in the jungle and made myself at home. I made a fire in one of the sites and cooked up a pail of oatmeal and along with some hard rolls, I had a good meal. I had to wait for a train to come in and that is why I went over to the town and was standing on a corner. This man came by in a nice car and stopped. He said, "Get in the car; I'm going to give you a good meal. We were supposed to have company come for dinner and they never showed up so we have a lot of leftovers." I told him that I had just had a little to eat down in the jungle but he wouldn't take no for an answer, so I got in the car, packsack and all, and he drove to his home. He had a really nice home with a large screened porch on the back. He and his wife were really nice folks. They set up a table on the porch and told me to start eating. A chicken dinner with all the trimmings, pie for dessert, I ate till I nearly busted at the seams. If I hadn't eaten not too long ago, back down in the jungle, I could have eaten more but they were satisfied and he took me back close to the railroad yard and left me off. I thanked him a lot and always remembered him as he was the only man to pick me up and take me to a real banquet.

"When our freight train came in and headed west, I climbed on an oil tank car and rode the first twenty miles. When the train stopped an old darkey walked by and said, "Boy, there's an empty box car a ways back." I went back and when I was crawling into the boxcar, who did I see but Glen. He had beaten me to it and had gotten on forty miles before I did. There were thirty of us in the car. Some were regular tramps who hadn't worked for twenty years and who went out of their way to get out of work. We stopped at one city about eight at night. It was a division city and the train didn't leave for nearly an hour. All the bums rushed for town trying to beg a bite to eat. The law stopped Glen and me but when we told them we had money they left us go. We rode most of the night."

To say the least that was the surprise of my life when I threw my packsack up in the box car and climbed in and looking and seeing Glen sitting in the middle of all those bums. He was sure glad to see me and we had a lot to talk over. The times when the train stopped and we went over to the town, we would hunt up a bakery and go in and ask for a dime's worth of old rolls, hard rolls, or even bread. Old rolls were better than fresh, they kept better in our packsacks and when we soaked them in cocoa or water, they were good eating. A can of beans and rolls made a good meal.

Usually every empty boxcar on the train had from a few to a lot of hoboes in it, all kinds: Negroes, Mexicans, young and old. At one stop even a man with his wife got into our boxcar and rode along. The lady was treated with great respect by everyone. When she had to go to the toilet, the man told us to all turn our heads, which we did. Then he would throw a bunch of papers out of the car. The travelers were dressed in all kinds of clothes, mostly what they picked up or scrounged in some way along the way. Most of the darkeys would have on a fairly heavy jacket.

Most of them had a knife of some kind in the pocket; several just carried old paring knives, like you see in a kitchen. Clothes lines along freight train routes were one source of getting fresh clothes.

One young man in particular was outstanding. When he unfolded his carryon bag he came up with a very large ladies heavy nightgown. I don't think the lady who lost it from her clothes line was very happy but the young man made good use of it each night. When he put it over his clothes at night to keep warm he looked like a big, striped, white ghost in the box car. This young man was a great talker and was always bragging about where he had been and what he had done. One evening we were riding along in the boxcar and he started bragging about all the women he took out in one night. He got through with his story and Glen spoke up and said, "Sonny, I think you better put your nightgown on now, and go to bed." All the hoboes got quite a laugh out of that. Sonny took it good naturedly and before long he was dressed for the night.

May 15, 1933, Monday.

"We held the train down all day across the prairie and desert of Northern Texas. I got an awful bawling out for asking a brakeman when our train left. I didn't think it was possible for any species of the human race to burst into such a fury as the brakeman did up in the panhandle of Texas. I may be mistaken for perhaps this wasn't a human being at all; at least he had no resemblance to one when he answered my simple question. Our private train had stopped at a small division town, out on the plains and while a couple of switch engines were tearing up and putting together a train, Glen and I dropped in at the local store. After purchasing a can of beans and a loaf of bread we walked back to the rail yards. To find our westward train was a question so upon seeing a breakie, I walked up and asked, "Is this our train you are making up?" Like an explosion, his huge frame fairly shook. He jerked his head down so as to get a dirty look with his fiery, snaky eyes, at me. The claw hammer he held, waved wildly in the air; his mouth opened so wide that his face disappeared and all I could see was long, stained yellow teeth. Then he roared out, trying to drown out the railroad engine interference, which he succeeded in doing. "Jesus Christ, you God damned sonofa****** can't you see what we're doing, now you dirty ****, when we get this train together, then get on and God damn you, maybe not then!" I thanked him for the information and we strolled off to look for the train he had so kindly informed us of.

I wouldn't consider taking most of northern Texas as a gift. About ten o'clock at night we got to El Paso. We couldn't ride in the yards because of the bulls. Our train left in a hurry so we just had time to walk around the yard and catch our train on the other side and on the run. I stumbled over a light and nearly broke my knee cap. I got in one car but the train was going too fast for Glen to get in that car and he got one further back. I had to sleep with a bunch of darkeys and Mexicans all night. The darkeys built a fire in the car. My knee hurt so I didn't sleep any all night."

May 16 and 17, 1933.

"In the morning I found Glen again. We crossed New Mexico and over the mountains and desert to Tucson, Arizona. We stayed on the freight train night and day. In the day time we would roast to death from the heat on the desert and at night we would freeze. About two hundred fellows were on our train. The bulls chased us out one night but we walked around and got on again. When we crossed the mountains in California we found a different country. Some of the fruit trees were filled with yellow oranges. In the evening we pulled into Los Angeles. We expected to get picked up by the railroad dicks and get put in the pen for two days but we jumped off before we got in the yard and went into the city. It's a very cheap city to live in. We got a room for fifty cents and good meals, from soup to dessert with everything, for ten cents."

Los Angeles was really quite a city for us to visit. We walked all over the main business district, went to ten cent movies at night, often saw two movies as they ran double features. The business district was filled with Chinese. They ran the restaurant where we ate the ten cent meals: four course, soup, salad, meat and potatoes and pie. Hock shops were all over, and it looked like most anything we wanted to buy was in the windows. One long barber shop advertised hair cuts from ten to twenty-five cents. Ten to twelve barbers worked, and each had his own chair. Those in the back were the beginners in barbering and they charged ten cents, up to the front of the shop were the professionals and they charged a quarter. It looked to me like most of the business was in the back.

May 18, 1933. "I packed my things this morning and left for Catalina Island but I got down to the dock late and missed my boat. Only one boat leaves at ten o'clock each day. I have to go through Long Beach over to Wilmington to catch the boat. The last earthquake certainly wrecked the buildings in Long Beach. It seems as if every building is having some repair work done on it. Lots of the large buildings are a complete wreck.

When I was headed back to Los Angeles I heard of a man wanting to hire some fellows. I hunted him up and he wanted us to sell oranges from house to house and work on a commission. I told him that Glen and I would be back later. When I saw Glen he objected to that kind of work. We saw two good shows at night for ten cents. They were a couple years old but o.k. We made final arrangements to split up tomorrow and meet in Salt Lake City."

I didn't mention in my diary or log book that Glen and I had decided to split, I wanted to go to Catalina Island where I had heard that Wrigley kept a young ball team, just to play for entertainment of the visitors. I had in mind that maybe I could get on the team and spend the summer. I had my catcher's mitt along in my packsack. Glen had in mind going north and then back to Western Montana where he had worked on a ranch a couple years back. He found the climate just right for his asthma in the dry climate there. We figured that later in the fall we would meet in Salt Lake City and go on from there. Glen was going to stay an extra day or so at the same hotel, so I had no trouble finding him. When I got back to his hotel I had all the oranges I could hold in my packsack. The man who wanted us to sell oranges took me back in a large garage and showed me some cots we could sleep on at night, meals we had to buy on our own. When I told him that we would probably start work in the morning, he left for other business. I sat on one of the cots for a while then thought to myself that I wanted to go to Catalina, not be tied up here, so I filled my pack with oranges and started back to find Glen. That was the first selling job I ever had, but I quit before I started.

May 19, 1933.

"I left early this morning for the island and Glen is going to head north to Frisco and over to Utah. He wrote home to have his clothes sent to Salt Lake. I bought a round trip ticket for one dollar and seventy-five cents and got on the steamer, all set for a thirty mile ride out in the

Pacific. The ride was wonderful. The coast was filled with U.S. warships and trading vessels. I could just see the island from the mainland. As we came closer it looked like a mountain top rearing its head out of the water. We anchored in a small harbor by the city of Avalon, nestled in between the hills, the only town on the island with rough mountain tops and hills all around. The island was bought by Wrigley in 1914 and he made his home here and made the island famous. Zane Grey has his home here and many other noted people.

About a year ago Mrs. Wrigley presented the island with a $25,000 clock, made with bells that would ring every fifteen minutes. The clock was close to Zane Grey's home and it kept him awake all night, so he got mad and left and only comes back occasionally.

As soon as I landed I walked up and looked at the Cub field. The young Cubs aren't here yet but will be here next Monday. I expect to wait and try out. I looked around and found a job for my room and board for the next few days. I have a job of doing the house cleaning in an apartment."

After leaving the baseball field I walked back down town and going by the first little eating place I walked in. The sign outside said, "Miss Grady's Home Dining Room, all you can eat for 50 cents." I went in and Miss Grady was sitting there and I told her I was looking for work. She was a very nice old lady, probably in her sixties, very gray, slim as a broom and looked like she was on the sickly side. I visited with her for a while, told her where I was from and how I was traveling. She was interested and then she told me she had a five or six room apartment and if I wanted to keep it cleaned up and do other odd jobs, I could have room and get board for nothing. That was a stroke of good luck to find a place to stay on my first inquiry. Also, she said when the Cubs come in; I could go up to the ball park in the afternoons.

She closed up the restaurant and we walked several blocks through town, then up a steep hill and there were five or six small building all hooked together. Each one had a bed, toilet, wash basin and chairs, just the necessities for overnight guests. They were built on split levels and from outside, we had a gorgeous view of the ocean.

She gave me one room for myself and went over the jobs I was to do. I felt like I was in heaven, to have a place like that to sleep in and know where my meals were coming from."

May 20, 1933. Saturday.

"I worked like hell all day cleaning and fixing up the apartments."

May 21, 1933. Sunday.

"I worked all forenoon painting the kitchen. I went for a wonderful hike in the afternoon. I followed a horse trail up to the top of the mountain. There I could see the Pacific on the other side and I had a good view of the country. The whole island is just one mountain after another. There are many tropical plants growing on the hills. I saw lots of new birds and I followed the wild goat trails over the hills. The island seems to be made up of soft crumbly rock and clay. No doubt in time it will be worn smooth and the ocean will swallow it up.

In the evening I met a jewelry man and had a good visit with him. He told me about a ray which he is working on and which he has invented. It only affects steel. It makes steel lose its magnetic property or a magnet won't attract it and it loses 43% of its weight. I saw some steel he experimented on. He gets his ray something like this. He runs electricity through a strong coil then through an ex-ray tube then through a prism. When the light is separated into three parts, he has a steel band that makes one dark and that is his strong ray."

May 22, 1933. Monday.

"The Catalina Cubs came in today, on the boat to stay for the summer. I went up to see the manager, Roy Johnson, and he is going to get a suit for me and I will work out tomorrow. I worked all day, still cleaning up the apartments."

May 23, 1933. Tuesday.

"I went up at two o'clock and got a Cub uniform and had a good work out. I think that I am the youngest in the bunch. They all seem to be experienced players. I would have a terrible hard time to break in to their team but I am going to try to work it so I can stay around and practice.

I found out this afternoon that I was the answer to a lady's prayer. The same day that I got this job with Miss Grady, she said that she found herself in trouble with all the work to do and she didn't know where or who to get to help her. She said she went upstairs, knelt down by her bed and said a special prayer, asking God to send her someone to help her. In about an hour I came along and God had directed me to her place. Miss Grady knows a man who is going to speak to Wrigley about me and try to help me with the ball team."

The park where the Cubs play is up a valley, probably five or six blocks from the Grady dining room. It's a nice diamond between the hills, has bleachers in back of the catcher's place and down both sides for a ways. No admission is charged, the team is kept there for the entertainment of the local people and the visitors.

They have a nice clubhouse, dressing rooms and showers. The players all stay in a dorm style home next to the clubhouse. The players are all paid some kind of a salary so they are set for the summer. I sure enjoyed the showers after each game. After each game I would go back to the dining room, maybe there would be some work to do there, otherwise, back to the apartments, painting and cleaning.

May 24, 1933.

"I cleaned house till twelve o'clock then I got in a suit and we had our first game today with a Los Angeles team. We had a very good game 4 to 3 in our favor. I didn't play any but I got a lot of good practice. Miss Grady's helper, Joe Davis came in to help for a while. Her cousin Emma is here too, for her health. We went for a walk after supper up along the beach. Some fishermen were along the boardwalk, all were having fishermen's luck except one and he had a sand shark which looked nearly like a mud catfish."

May 25, 1933

"I got a good workout with the boys today. I get to do all the catching in the warming up. They call me "The Kid" around the diamond. We beat some movie production team today, 5 to 2.

Joe and I are still busy cleaning house. The climate is certainly wonderful here. The sun shines all day and it doesn't get too hot because it's so damp. In the evening it is cool and at night we use five or six blankets. When I first came here I found eight on my bed."

May 26, 1933.

"We beat a department store team today 7 to 0. Emma and I went for a walk in the evening up to Pebbly Beach and picked up a few strange shells."

May 27, 1933.

"We won our game today. I bought some lines and squid for bait, and Ed and I went fishing in the evening. I saw my first wild seal this evening. There were eight or ten playing around or fishing where I wanted to fish.

Last night I was in an earthquake but I didn't realize it and didn't know about it till today. It broke a window in one house. I woke up at the time but didn't know what had woke me."

May 28, 1933. Sunday.

"We had an eleven inning game and beat a Hollywood team 7 to 5. Miss Grady opened her café up today and served 19 people each a 50 cent dinner. She was well satisfied. The world fair opened up today in Chicago. There was plenty on the radio about it."

May 29, 1933. Monday.

"We laid off ball today. I heard from home. I varnished and painted all day. Miss Grady served four people today.

Miss Grady owns a lot of property on the island so we never run out of work. She has a nice home next to the café and the café is built out from the hill side and there are several rooms over and back of the dining room. Where I stay, she has 5 or 6 small buildings with from two to three rooms in each, all for rent.

Also, a small home nearby, is rented by the month to a man and wife. An apricot tree is in the back, loaded with fruit."

May 30, 1933.

"Lots of people came over to celebrate Decoration Day on the island. A boat came in last night with 350 on it and most of them were drunk. About midnight they all wanted black coffee. Nearly all the ball team fellows were across to the mainland for yesterday. You could tell by their playing today that something was the matter. They were all sluggish and could hardly move and they got trimmed 8 to 14. Johnson, the coach, was certainly sour. He sat on the bench and cussed a blue streak at each player. After he had covered the whole nine of them, he would start over."

May 31, 1933.

"I haven't been getting much practice lately so I'm going to quit baseball. I expect to hang around for a while and work for Miss Grady till I hear from Glen. She offered me $5 a week for the summer if I would stay and work for her."

June 1, 1933.

"I quit baseball and started working for Miss Grady. Joe Davis, the other helper and I have it pretty nice working here. We can get up when we want and cook anything we want for breakfast.

Then we can do what we want to, and work as hard as we want to, and stop when we want to, and go over to town. All in all it's a good place to work."

June 2, 1933.

"I heard from Glen today. He just got into Salt Lake City. He had caught a ride 320 miles south of San Francisco and made it all the way to Seattle. While in a café in Seattle, he had another fainting spell. He was out for six hours. That's the hardest one he's gotten yet. He bummed a freight train the last 600 miles into Salt Lake City. When I told Miss Grady about this, she immediately said she would give me five dollars to send him, so as to help him get in a good climate."

June 3, 1933.

"I got the five dollars and sent it to Glen. Today over a thousand of the American Legion men and their followers came over to celebrate. Nearly all of them were well stewed. They ran the town all day and will make merry most of the night."

June 4, 1933.

Sunday. "I got up at four o'clock this morning to hike out and see the wild goats. The street down town was still filled with young and old men. Some were hollering and raising hell, others were trying to remember where they lived.

I followed a road out to the mountain tops for six miles, when I saw my first wild goats. I started to circle down through the brush when I ran onto three that were so busy eating that they didn't see me. I got to within ten feet of a large brown shaggy buck. I had my camera set and when he raised his head and saw me I snapped him. He took one look at me and down over the mountain he went. I came across a herd of about forty, all sizes and colors. I chased them over one ridge after another trying to catch a lamb but they were all too fast.

I found a part of an old Indian stone bowl and a stone spearhead on one hill. Joe Davis left for Los Angeles today and probably for good. Miss Grady went over too, on business, so Emily and I have to run the café for a day or so."

The island is about twenty-two miles long by four miles wide in the widest place. The whole island was bought by William Wrigley in 1919 and he developed the area that surrounds Avalon. A poor dirt or rocky trail runs the length of the island. There were some fishermen living on the other side but I never got back that far. Too far to walk in one day and there is no hitchhiking on the trail. Wrigley built a beautiful home up on the mountain side overlooking Avalon and the harbor.

June 5, 1933. Monday.

"I heard from Rud today. He's going strong in baseball. I was the chef in the kitchen today and Emily the waitress. We served 12 customers."

Being the chief cook didn't bother me at all. I had worked in a cafeteria most of the previous winter for my meals while in school in Madison. It didn't take me too long to put out a meal, mostly meat that was already cut up; ready to cook, mashed potatoes and chicken that came cooked, rolled up in a crust and all we had to do was warm it up good and pour gravy over it. The gravy came in a paper cup container, put it in hot water for awhile, open it up and pour over the chicken. Our menu listed several kinds of fish: sea bass, barracuda, perch and one or two other native fish. We usually kept one kind of fresh fish in the icebox. If two customers came in and each one wanted a different kind of fish then I had to run out the back door, down the alley and a block over on Main Street to a fish market and buy a slab of the kind I needed. One of the tricks to the trade in the restaurant business was to have people sitting at the tables. It took time to run down and buy fish then get back and cook it up, lots of customers complained some about the slow service. They would be gone back on the boat and new customers would come in the next time, so we were never in a hurry to serve.

June 6,7,8,9, 1933.

"Miss Grady didn't get back until June 8. She got sick over in town and had to stay a while. Emma and I had the café running, but for three days straight now, we haven't had a customer. The ice was broken tonight when one customer came in. An elderly man came over from Los Angles to paper and help paint. I heard from Glen today and he has sold a few moth pads."

Mr. Johnson was the new worker, probably in his early seventies; quite small, frail looking man who has a great sense of humor and is always smoking a pipe. He is an old retired painter and paper hanger. Miss Grady had looked around Los Angeles for someone who could do this type of work and who wouldn't expect much pay. She found him willing to come over for a while, just for his room and board and tobacco money. He said he wanted to get out of the city for awhile because where he lived it was more or less an old folks home.

Glen wrote that he had started selling moth pads door to door trying to make some money. I had written home early in June and had my summer clothes sent out. Now I have white shirts, light pants and tennis shoes. I even had a suit coat and ties sent because in order to get in the Avalon Dance Pavilion customers had to have a coat and tie on. This huge Pavilion was built by Wrigley and they have famous orchestras come over to play. A board walk goes all along the coast line several blocks from down town Avalon. Admission is free, but everyone had to be dressed up to get in. Wrigley has it for the entertainment of the visitors and locals. Food and drinks are the only source of revenue.

June 10, 1933.

"Mr. Johnson started to paper. When we got some on the ceiling Miss Grady found that she didn't like the color of it. After whining and whimpering for an hour she decided to let it go. She went across to pick out the paper then she left it to someone else over there and now she blames him for not choosing what she likes."

June 11, 1933.

"I caught my first ocean fish today. Maybe I didn't hook it fair, as I hooked it in the eye and snaked it in. It was about a 1 ½ pound bass. I used squid for bait and got some other good yanks. Another fisherman gave me a bass and a perch which weighed about 1 ½ pounds."

I took these fish back to the café and cleaned them up. They made good sized fillets, not as neat as those we buy but I had often watched at the fish market how they cleaned fish so I did my best. Some customer eventually got them for lunch, whether they were served as ordered I doubt. No matter what kind the other customer ordered we served what we had in the ice box. Unless, as I had said before, if two different kinds of fish were ordered at the same table then I had to run out the back door, down the alley to the fish market and buy a different kind. Whenever I had time from then on I did quite a lot of fishing. In one place on the coast I could get out on the rocks and fish down in the really deep water. Mostly I caught what they called button perch; a nice looking, fairly thick fish, with a black dot on their tail. Back home we would classify them in the carp family but every good sized one I caught was served up as bass or some other kind, depending what was on our menu.

Miss Grady's Home Dining Room was known to have the best soup on the Island. There was a little trick to that too. In order to have good soup you have to start with good soup stock as it was called. All beef bones or leftover meat that came back into the kitchen and off the customer's plate was just added to the big soup kettle. The stock was good for several days, bring it to a good boil, add a pinch of soda and then we added our vegetables. Soup was plentiful and cheap and when we advertise, all you can eat for 50 cents, they started off with a very large bowl of Miss Grady's famous soup.

June 12&13, 1933.

"The carpenters are nearly through and it won't be long now till we are finished up. I go down to the beach at 11:30 for a swim each day, I rigged up a spear with a line attached and I expect to use it pretty soon."

Miss Grady had two carpenters doing some remodeling in several of her apartments. I often worked close by them, painting or cleaning up. Neither of them was an expert, but both thought they knew it all. One we called Mac. He was a large, fat man and from his talk you would think he was the most industrious worker in the world. Daily he would tell the story of how he would like to start work at five o'clock in the morning but the city officers wouldn't let him because of disturbing the citizen's sleep. The other would be carpenter, Charlie by name, was a foreigner. He was just the opposite of Mac, small, skinny, he started work late and quit early. One day I was working in a room next to where Charlie was fixing up a shower bathe. Mac happened to come along and look in on Charlie.

"Charlie, he said. "This shower will never do, it's too small." Then they went into a real argument.

Charlie---"Oh no, days plenty room here."

Mac--- "To hell there is, there is no room for your stool."

Charlie—"What stool is that?"

Mac---"Why the stool you sit on."

Charlie—"To hell you don't say, we don't sit on stools, when we take a shower."

Mac---"By god you do, all showers have stools, I've got one."

Charlie---"By Got day don't, I ain't got one in my place. What do you want to sit down for?"

Mac---"Why lots of people want to sit down and wash their feet."

Charlie---"Ta hell with yah, we lift up our feet and wash'um. You got such a big belly you need to sit down so to reach your feet."

That held Mac for the afternoon but at his quitting time he came around to Charlie and said, "Well, Charlie, we didn't do so much today but we'll certainly give her hell tomorrow."

There is a fine sandy beach just to the edge of Avalon and every day it is filled with sunbathers and swimmers. Girls and boys with just barely the necessary clothing lay around the beach for hours. The water is clear and they can wade out for a ways and then they are in really deep water. In twenty feet of water they can still see bottom. The pier where the big boats land is close by. Young swimmers would often swim out by the boats and dive for coins the tourists would throw in. Salt water is a lot easier to swim in than fresh. I spent a lot of time swimming around the rocks and looking at fish. I never did get a fish with my spear.

June 14 & 15, 1933.

"I heard from Glen and he is thinking of leaving Salt Lake and going up to Montana and getting a haying job. He sold $450 worth of moth pads. He's been too sick to sell much. He had a fainting spell in Seattle which knocked him out. Glen told me later on that when he was selling moth pads door to door in Salt Lake City, he walked up to a house and a big fat man opened the door. Glen explained his mission. There were some women in the room and the man wanted to show off so he got mad and said, "I want you to understand that when I find a moth in my house I swallow it." He started to walk away and Glen said, "Well, Mister, that's the healthiest way to do all right."

Miss Grady's niece came today; her name is Helen Nancy O'Malley, from Chicago. She is in her early twenties, very slim, medium height and full of life. She expects to stay for the summer and help Miss Grady."

June 16 to 22, 1933.

"Mr. Johnson and I have been painting and fixing up most of the time. We have a good time joshing one another about our pay and work. Glen is leaving for Deer Lodge, Montana where he will try for a haying job. I heard from Jack Harvey. He doesn't like the grub in the CCC Camp where he is at.

I went on the flying fish boat last night. They have a large light which flashes on the water and attracts the fish. Some sail for half a block or more. We saw thousands of them. Some would fly into the boat."

The flying fish boat goes out every night just after dark. Some folks even had small dip nets they carried and would try and net a fish in the air when it came close. The fish have long side fins which act as sails. When they get speed up to thirty miles per hour they come out of the water and glide like a bird. They are good eating and all were saved that were caught. The boat makes the trip up past the Avalon Dance Pavilion and it's quite a sight to be out in the water and see it all lighted up with colored lights.

June 22 to 30, 1933.

"Glen got to Deer Lodge okay and might work on a sheep ranch for a while. Mr. Johnson and I are still going strong. I'm working from early morning till late at night and I'm getting sick of it.

The rental units have been really busy, especially on weekends. Every morning after breakfast I clean the rooms, change the sheets and pillow cases and sweep up the walks. Those that come over to party leave quite a mess. Often the floor has to be mopped up. Laundry goes in a bag and some lady collects it each day and brings back the clean clothes. We lose quite a few towels."

July 1, 1933.

"I told Miss Grady I would quit if I didn't get more money. At first she said I had better go but when she saw I meant it, and then she raised me to seven dollars a week so I will stay a while."

July 2 to 7, 1933.

"Miss Grady got sick just before the fourth and I was the chef in the kitchen. I cooked up everything and served it. We had about 80 people a day.

There was a big crowd over on the night of July 3rd. Nearly all of them were drunk and raised hell all night. There wasn't much doing on the fourth because they were all sobering up. I had to work seventeen hours in the kitchen on the fourth."

We had to fill up the crowds over the holidays on beef, fish and chicken. Some ordered T bone steaks, so we had a lot of good bones to add to the soup stock. Helen and Emily did most of the waiting on tables and dish washing. I made a few fast trips to the fish market. Whatever fish we had on hand, that's what they got, no matter what they ordered and no one knew the difference. Good, strong, black coffee went over big from morning until late at night. A few left ten cent tips, once in a while a quarter so the girls were satisfied. Miss Grady gets terrible headaches that nearly lays her up.

July 8, 1933.

Sunday. "Well, I had to work all day fixing up an apartment. I'm getting tired of working all the time. Mr. Johnson and I hit upon an idea today which we expect to try. We plan on buying an old car over in Los Angeles and loading up his painting outfit and traveling from town to town and do sign painting and any other kind of painting or wall papering. I'm going to tell Miss Grady that I won't stay for less than twelve dollars a week and which she won't pay, which I am sure of, and then I will go over and see Mr. Johnson."

I learned a lot from Mr. Johnson. He showed me how to use a paint brush, how to grain doors and how to hang wall paper. One thing he said, "If you contract a job then spread the paint on thick and brush it out thin that will make the paint go further."

July 8 to 15, 1933.

"I'm still working from morning till night. Mr. Johnson left the other day for Los Angeles. I threatened to leave the other day and Miss Grady got up a whole new story, so I'm staying for a while. She wants me to take over the café in the fall by October and run it fifty-fifty during the fall and take care of her places this winter. If Glen could stand the climate I would consider it but I think I will be leaving shortly. I just heard from Glen and he left Montana and he didn't know for sure which way he was headed."

I had been on the island for quite a while. Had most all of my wages saved up, made quite a bank roll, besides my feet were itching to travel and hook up with Glen someplace.

July 16-17, 1933.

"I heard from Glen. He's around Dillon, Montana trying for a haying job. I'm leaving on Wednesday. Miss Grady hates to see me go.

July 18, 1933.

"I packed up today and took some last pictures of the island. Austin O'Malley and Miss Grady's sister came today from Chicago. We knew Austin was coming but we didn't know Miss Grady's sister was coming. She walked in later and surprised Miss Grady nearly to death."

I had quite a busy day packing. I wanted my camping outfit and clothes, camera and small items all to fit in my pack sack. The rest of my clothes I sent back home. I wrote home that I would be leaving and intended to find Glen someplace. Austin is Helen's brother and he intends to stay on the island for a while and help Miss Grady with all the work. Ernie had left a while back for the mainland but he came back a few days ago and is helping with the apartments.

July 19, 1933.

"There was a royal time this morning as I left. The girls got breakfast and when I left for the boat Babe (Emily) got the mouth organ, Emma the guitar and Ernie the violin. They were going down to the boat and play music as I left. I talked to a traveling salesman on the boat over. I found Mr. Johnson's apartment at the Mann Hotel and put up with him. Austin gave me a ticket on the Southern Pacific Railroad to San Francisco. I'll leave Friday morning on it.

I had some trouble with some Jews over a watch they sold me which wouldn't run. I told them in plain language what I thought of them."

I really hated to leave the island and the nice folks I was working with. The musicians came down to the boat and they kept playing all the time I walked up the gang plank. They were still on the dock waving as the boat pulled out to sea. All summer long several big boats were going between the island and the mainland. I still had my return ticket which was good for my way back.

July 20, 1933. "I looked the city over today and went out to Hollywood and looked around. It's not so hot out there. There are lots of beautiful homes. I saw the studios but I couldn't get inside. We took in a show tonight."

Traveling was easy around the cities. Streetcars run from one city to the next. Just keep asking which car to take and before long you were there. Hills and mountains surround most of the city. Somewhere back of Hollywood I found a road that went up in the mountains. I followed that a long way up then left the road and cut across the hills and looked out over the whole city. I took a short cut down out of the mountains and when I got to the bottom everything was fenced in. This didn't bother me too much; I climbed over a chain link fence right into the backyard of one of these fancy homes. Guess no one was home as I walked through their yard out onto the street. I had a good day, lots to see, lots of hiking, found Mr. Johnson smoking his pipe. We had a lot to talk over but we forgot all about buying a car and looking for painting jobs.

July 21, 1933.

"I said, 'So long,' to Mr. Johnson at the Mann Hotel on Olive Street and I went down and got on my train to Frisco. There was no trouble about my ticket and I had a nice ride up the coast to Frisco. We crossed the Sierra Madre Mountains and traveled up valleys and along the coast. I saw oil wells dug out in the ocean, also a Chinese ship on the rocks left there for the waves to take to pieces. I got to Frisco at 8:30 pm and got a twenty-five cent hotel room. The city isn't as nice as L.A."

July 22, 1933.

"I slept late, then went out and looked the city over. It's pretty hilly and lots of foreigners. I went down to the harbor and found I had to take a ferry to Oakland. On the ferry I got a distant view of the Golden Gate Bridge. It was pretty cloudy and lots of dirty foreign ships were filling it up.

I got a ride with a man headed for Sacramento. I thought I would go over there and try for work in the fruit valley. A man told me there was work to be had at Winter, about twenty five miles from Sacramento. I got off and walked ten miles over the foot hills to Winter but all the work was over with. It got very hot in the afternoon. The other day it was 108 degrees but today it is only 98 above. I found a grain field where there were some bundles of straw and I put up there for the night."

San Francisco is built alongside a mountain. The good harbor is what makes the city run. Boats or ships from all nations were docked or either coming or going. I spent some time all along the waterfront. Fish houses were scattered all along the shoreline. Some places would be cleaning fish, other places selling fish. The smell was something, I even smelt like fish after being at the waterfront for awhile. Horse delivery wagons were all over, cut meats were dirty and flies covered anything that was still. Tough looking sailors and foreigners were all crowded together. There would be several languages spoken, seemed like all at the same time, by the people working the waterfront. Ships were loading and unloading and after several hours, I was ready to keep traveling.

July 23, 1933.

"It got pretty cold last night and I had to gather other piles of straw to get under. I walked till 3 o'clock in the afternoon before I got a ride. I walked by acres of orchards. There are olive groves, English walnuts and many other fruits. I got into Sacramento, the capitol of California about five o'clock. It is a beautiful capitol. There is a park surrounding the capitol which has hundreds of different trees from all over the world.

The town is filled with Japs. I got a hotel room for 35 cents from a Jap down in the Jap district. I have a bad cold and don't feel so hot."

July 24, 1933.

"There was no mail for me today. I started in business for myself today. I tried the stamp racket that Glen told me about. I made $1.10 and a good meal by mowing a lawn."

We had a system of getting our mail ever so often. I would write home and to Glen and tell them some city that I would probably be in before long. They would send a letter marked

"General Delivery, hold for 30 days." This system worked really well and we usually got our mail sometime before it would be returned.

The stamp business, as we called it, was a sure fire business. It usually paid out but I had to work at it. I would go up to a house, ring the bell or knock and when someone came I started talking really fast; go through a list of jobs to do, mow the lawn, trim the hedge, wash windows, clean the chicken coop, and if they had one of any other chores I could think of. I expected them to say, "No." which most of them did, then I'd tell them I needed a job so I could buy a stamp so I could write a letter home. If women answered the door they most always said, "Wait, I'll go and get a stamp for you." Some gave me one and some would give me several and at two cents each, they counted up. After twenty-five to fifty knocks on doors, I had a fair day's wages. Stamps could always be changed for cash at most taverns or hotels.

On one side street I went up to a home and knocked and an older lady came out. She heard my lingo on jobs and asked me where I was from. I told her, "From Wisconsin," and her face lit up and she said she came from Wisconsin years before. Her husband and another lady lived in this place and they seemed really pleased to have a Wisconsin visitor. She said I could mow the lawn which I did and then they set me up to a really good meal and a quarter for the extra work. They were really nice and later on, every time I got back to Sacramento I would head for their home the first thing.

July 25, 1933.

"I thought I would put in another days work at the stamp game. The first house I stopped at had a job for me. I washed windows for three hours at 25 cents an hour. In the afternoon I made 75 cents in the stamp racket. I took in a dime show tonight. It was run by Japs and the people were all Japs or darkeys."

In the morning I made one man really angry. I knocked at his door and when he came out and saw me, did he ever cuss. He said, "You were here yesterday, you bum, get going and don't come around my house again." Each day I worked side streets or the residential areas. Often I forgot which street I had worked until someone let me know about it. One lady had a job; she had a three story house and asked how much I would take to wash the windows way up on the third floor. I looked the house over good and decided I didn't want any part of climbing so high, so I told her I would have to have 35 cents per hour for that job. I knew it would be too high which it was, so I kept going.

July 26, 1933.

"I followed the stamp racket for a while but I didn't do so well, I did lots of chasing around and made 76 cents. I gave up my hotel room and slept in a park. Another young fellow was with me and we were entertained till one o'clock at night by some girls and boys who were throwing a party across the street. The girls got pretty well plastered and they went out to play on the lawn."

The park we slept in was the big park around the capitol. It had lots of large evergreen trees with branches protruding outward and down to the ground. After dark we picked out a tree and climbed under the branches and no one would ever find us there. We spread out our canvas and we're right at home.

July 27, 1933.

"No mail yet, so I hit the highway north to Marysville where I heard there was work in the orchards. They hadn't started picking yet. I tried the stamp racket but it wouldn't work in a small town.

One man got awful sore because I got him out of bed to ask him to mow his lawn. I got on the highway again and decided to pass my time up on the Feather River and make a circle over to Reno, Nevada. I'm camping at Oroville in a little park beside the Feather River. I'm up near the hills now and the country is much greener. All along the river gold mining machines tear up the gravel after the gold."

July 28, 1933.

"I left Oroville, and expected a good walk over the mountains to Quincy. I bought two pounds of raisins and started out. I walked nearly all day over the hills and mountains. I took a side road three miles back in the hills to look for a job in a lumber camp. I climbed to an altitude of 6,500 feet. I rode with one lady who was pretty careless in making the curves. I got into Quincy at night. I tried sleeping in a flat car with a metal bottom but I froze out. Then I found an empty coach. I opened the door and heard someone snoring. I thought someone was using it as a bedroom. I sneaked around with my flashlight and found the sleeper. It was another bum on the floor covered from head to foot with a blanket."

July 29, 1933.

"When I hit Nevada I hit another desert. The hills are rounded from a glacier, covered with rock, sage brush and cactus. Outside of Reno I saw the Alkali Lake. It's hard and used as a race track. Reno is known as the "Biggest Little Town in the World". It probably is. Saloons are wide open and gambling is too. I was looking for a place to sleep when I saw what appeared to be a deserted house with a hay stack beside it. I went up and found two old men lived there. They gave me a chicken supper and a bed in the straw. They said I could hay for them on their ranch for a day or so. I asked them how large a ranch he had. He said, "Well, I own about six acres of my own but I rent another twenty."

Jim Shannon was the owner of the ranch and Homer was the cook. Jim was a fairly stout man, always had on high boots, large black hat and quite a beard. Homer was a small dried up little old man. Bald headed, always had a homemade cigarette dangling from his lips. He was the cook and dish washer. Both men were really fine, good natured fellows. Not always too clean but I wasn't either. Their house and other buildings were up on a bench maybe a block above the road. I could see only the house and other small buildings from the road. The whole place looked deserted until you walked up the grade and got to the house. A small creek came down from the valley above, close to the house, that's where Homer got all his wash water. A large gravel bank was on the other side of the road, maybe twenty feet or higher making up the hill. An open face showed gravel was being taken out. Toward the back were a small barn, bunk house, tool shed and odds and ends of small buildings. He kept a team of horses, a nice black saddle horse, four of five cows, a few pigs and some chickens. All in all it looked like a going ranch once you looked it over.

July 30, 1933.

"Sunday today but I worked all day haying and cutting up wood. A man by the name of Ernie worked with me this morning. Last night he said he tried to get drunk on beer. He drank twenty glasses and was still sober so he came up here and went to bed."

Homer uses a lot of wood in his kitchen stove and Jim has a large cast iron kettle hanging over a fire place up by his pig pen. He keeps a fire going there boiling up all different vegetables and any old meats for his hogs. He has a relative in a store down in Reno and gets lots of fruit and potatoes, and other vegetables that go bad. All goes into the big iron kettle for hog feed.

July 31, 1933.

"I put up some more hay today and cut more wood. I eat so much here that I can hardly work. I walked into Reno tonight and looked around. Gambling is going on left and right. I could hear poker chips clatter clear out in the street. They play Bingo with a pot of from forty to one hundred dollars. They all seem to like it here."

The doors were always wide open in front of the gambling places. I walked in several and just looked around. Tables would be full of card players, chips passing back and forth. I didn't understand any of the games, some slot machines were busy, some kind of a racing program was tilted on the wall and letters were being changed. Looked like the race or something was

over and a man with an eraser rubbed off numbers and chalked new ones up. If I spent any money it would be for a large bottle of pop and a five cent, quarter pound candy bar.

August 1, 1933.

"I'm still holding on to this large ranch. We put up another jig of hay then I got up a setting of wood. I went up to a canyon and broke off willow trees and trimmed them with my hands. I had a shotgun along to shoot ground squirrels. I heard a noise in the brush and a coyote jumped out. I shot and he fell dead. He was about two-thirds grown. While I was cutting wood a hearse came down over the hillside like a bat out of hell to the paupers' graveyard and buried a stiff."

There was an irrigation ditch that ran all along the top of Jim's rented ranch. Water is drained from the ditch down on Jim's hay and wheat fields. Above the ditch is sage brush and rock and up on top of a hill there is a nice, well kept, graveyard. Down the hill, across a ravine and up the other side, right in the brush and rock, they have what they call the paupers' graveyard. Derelicts and those without money or family are buried there. No ceremony or nothing, just a shallow hole and a cheap coffin goes in and a marker put up, sometimes with a name and sometimes marked, name unknown. It was common to see the old truck of a hearse go down the hill and up to this rocky brushy patch, dig down a ways and leave someone there. Once in a while the truck would go down empty, dig up someone and take off for the city. When they found the identity of someone and he didn't belong there he was dug up and shipped off. From where I often worked, I could see funerals going on up above. I went up several times and picked up several pairs of thin gloves that the pall bearers always wore then discarded them on the way out.

August 2-3-4-5, 1933.

"I'm doing up all the odd jobs around here. Our friend Ernie came around this morning and told us how he and another fellow blew up a cave with five sticks of dynamite and got three pups and the mother coyote. Mr. Johnson paid me tonight for the weeks work. He gave me five silver dollars and four, fifty cent pieces. That's a load itself to carry around."

Lots of days in the afternoon Jim would tell me to go up in the hills and shoot some jack rabbits for the pigs. I usually walked up a ravine that had really steep sides. Jacks would jump up, head up the hillside and when I shot, they would roll back down. I usually got down two to five jacks on each hunt. Five would be all I could drag back down through the brush to the boiling kettle. All were thrown into the kettle and boiled up with whatever else Jim had in it. The hogs really liked all the meat cooked that way. One day I shot a big quail from a tree by the barn; it went into the pot too, for hog feed.

August 6, 1933.

"Worked half a day, then went for a hike up in the mountains. I found some old gold or silver mines. They were caves or holes in the ground."

I always had my high leather boots on when working or hiking. I never knew when I would see a rattlesnake. I killed several small ones but no real old timers.

August 7-8-9, 1933.

"We're cutting wheat. Mr. Shannon cuts it with a mower, then rakes it with a dump rake and then I put it in piles. I worked only half a day today and yesterday. I went into Reno in the afternoon and took in a show."

August 10 to 14, 1933.

"We're still tinkering around. I expect to finish up tomorrow, and then I expect to hit the freights and do some traveling. It's pretty warm here. The thermometer went up to 112 the other day. A man gave Jim a half pint of whiskey for a dozen ears of sweet corn tonight.

Homer thinks Jim and I are heavy eaters. A gallon dish of pudding lasts us two for only two meals. Also, we use up from ten to twelve lemons a day. Homer said we drank four gallons of lemonade the other day."

August 15, 1933.

"We worked half a day and finished up. I'm staying over until tomorrow morning then I'll head west."

August 16, 1933.

"I rode with Mr. Shannon in his horse and cart into town. He scares me to ride with him; we nearly got hit three different times. I walked three miles out in the country to a ranch but no job.

Then I went down to Sparks and at one thirty I got a freight. Two other fellows and I rode on top of a fruit car. There was beautiful scenery crossing the Sierra Nevada Mountains. It rained hard so we had to get down in the chuck hole where they put the ice. We passed through tunnels and snow sheds. About eleven o'clock we got into Roseville, fifteen miles from Sacramento. The whole train stopped there so I slept the rest of the night in the ice hole. One fellow who was with me always wanted to steal something. At first he wanted to get off the train and steal a chicken, and then up in Truckee where we saw a herd of sheep, he wanted to hide in the willows and grab a lamb when it went by."

August 17, 1933.

"I woke up and found an engine had hooked on my car at night and pulled me down in the storage lot. I had to walk two miles out. First thing I saw was my two friends of the day before, one was in an orchard and garden.

A local train wasn't to leave until ten o'clock, so I hitchhiked into Sacramento. I got my mail. I heard from Glen and had to laugh when he told about the poor grub where he worked. I'm going down and see Jack Harvey then probably head north. I hitchhiked into Stockton and it took me almost all afternoon. This morning I hunted up the ladies in Sacramento for whom I had trimmed a hedge once before. I got a good feed and twenty cents. I also got about thirty big peaches off their tree. It made for a big load for me.

It's just seven o'clock now and I'm going to take a freight out of here south tonight at eleven thirty. I'm writing down in the jungle and there are lots of other tough looking fellows around.

I had a good laugh today when I read Jack Harvey's card. I asked him for directions and all he said was, "Why in hell didn't you come down here when you were in Reno? If you don't come on down now, I'll knock hell out of you."

My peaches got soft and ran all over everything in my pack. I'm trying to eat them up now."

The ladies in Sacramento seemed really pleased to see me again. Being from Wisconsin sure made the difference. I mowed their lawn and trimmed the hedge, and then had a really good meal. They insisted on me filling my pack with peaches and giving me two dimes.

All the hard cash I had changed into paper money and all of that was hid in my money belt. I always wore a tee shirt under my shirt to hide the belt. If some of the bums knew I had money on me, I would have been rolled for sure.

August 18, 1933.

"I slept for a while last evening and then at eleven o'clock I got up to catch my train. It didn't show up until nearly two o'clock, and then it was going too fast for me to jump. I crawled in a box car and slept till morning. Some trains were to leave in the morning but I didn't see them and so at nine, I got mad and started hitchhiking south.

After walking through the hot valley I finally got a ride with a truck driver in the middle of the afternoon. He was hauling nearly eight tons of apples to Fresno. It was an old relic of a truck, all hard tires. It was terrible to drive because I drove several hours. The driver said if he could sell his apples and get some more orders he would give me a job of helping drive and load. I went into Fresno with him and we finally got in late at night."

August 19, 1933.

"We started out in the morning to get rid of his apples. We went all forenoon from one buyer to another and all the stores but they all had plenty. We tried to get a spot on Market Street and market them but we were too late. He thought he would go home for the weekend then market them next Tuesday. He couldn't rent a motorcycle so he bought an old Dodge truck for twelve dollars and two boxes of apples.

He drove the apple truck in a storage garage and broke through some planks over a grease pit. The wheel went way in and spilt apples all over hell. We worked until twelve o'clock that night and finally got the apples loaded and packed and the truck in shape."

August 20, 1933.

Sunday. "The job didn't look too promising to me besides it was too dangerous driving. We nearly got smashed into several times. The driver couldn't go home so he took me to the next little town and then I started hitchhiking to Merced. Then I turned east for the Yosemite National Park and over to see Jack Harvey at Leevining.

I got a ride with a truck into Merced. It's all grapes and fruit in the valley. I saw the largest peach orchard in the world at Merced, over 7,000 acres. A very talkative man picked me up headed into Yosemite Valley. He drove fast and I rode in the park with him. The mountains going into the park were beautiful to drive over. We dropped 4,000 feet on one hill then over another mountain and down in the valley of Yosemite. The valley is really wonderful. A fast, small, river with lots of rapids cuts through it while towering cliffs of granite rear their heads hundreds of feet in the air. It's a real canyon. I left the car to take a side road in my direction. I made camp beside the road in the pines. It was warm at first but in the night I had to cover up with pine needles. There are lots of bear around here but none bothered me last night."

August 21, 1933.

"After looking a map over I found that I could take a trail out of the end of the valley over to my highway to Leevining; so I started down the main Yosemite Canyon or valley. On both sides the cliffs are from 2,000 to 3,000 feet high. The waterfalls are pretty well dried up now.

I met with a brown bear and two black cubs. I was trying to herd them together to get a picture and the old mother came after me. About ten feet from me she waved her paw at me and I beat it but I got the picture. I got rides down to Clear Lake and then I took a trail thirteen miles long to Lake Lenania which is on the highway. To get out of the valley I had to climb a mountain just about straight up. The path zig zagged a thousand times to the summit and it took me three hours to make it up. There was lots of wild game.

I reached the lake at 4 o'clock and caught a ten mile ride to the Meadows camp. I was just going up in the brush to look for a sleeping place when out walked a big bear. A little farther on I made camp. The elevation is 9,000 feet here and snow is on the mountains. There were no pine needles so I put sticks up beside a log and crawled under. At twelve o'clock I froze out and started hiking to keep warm. I came to a mess of fires and three men were tending them. At two o'clock we had coffee and lunch and I slept beside a fire the rest of the night."

August 22, 1933.

"I took a bath and cleaned up in an icy stream at six o'clock this morning. I got rides into Leevining and found where Jack Harvey was. Jack doesn't like the camp very well. He's a boss over a gang of men. Jack couldn't get off, so I got permission to stay with Jack. The chow didn't taste bad to me. It's an awful noisy place, especially at the table. The fellows don't hurt themselves working and they use plenty of rough language."

These CCC camps were put in by President Roosevelt to give work to thousands of young men who were out of work. They were paid twenty dollars a month which most was sent home to their folks. There must have been seventy-five to one hundred men in this camp doing some kind of forest work: making roads, dams, planting trees or cleaning up parks.

August 23, 1933.

"While Jack was working today I climbed up a big mountain back of camp. I came across a patch of snow and I made a face in it out of big rocks. It was about forty feet across and I could see it for a long ways. I caught a hell of a cold in the snow too."

August 24, 1933.

"I left the camp this morning and had pretty good luck catching rides into Reno. A man and two ladies picked me up and when they stopped they gave me two bucks. I found Mr. Shannon and Homer OK.

August 25, 1933.

"I worked around the ranch this forenoon and worked for a neighbor this afternoon."

August 26 to 31, 1933.

"I worked for two days and a half for Joe Williams and he gave me two dollars a day. Mr. Shannon has some work for me here so I'm hanging around."

Joe Williams had a little farm under irrigation down in the valley below Jim's ranch. He used a large wooden wheel with buckets and troughs. As the stream turned the wheel, the water was carried up to the top in the buckets and spilled over in a large trough and then moved down to his fields. The wheel was probably thirty feet tall and about six feet wide. A lot of the paddles were broken and frames needed replacing. All made out of wood and was fixed so it could be shut off. I climbed all over the wheel with a hammer and nails and replaced what needed fixing. Mr. Williams stayed on the bank, telling me what to do and not to fall off and into the creek.

September 1 to 12, 1933.

"I'm doing a little of everything for Jim. We drained an irrigation lake and are going to clean it. I'm fixing up a barn and moving a fence."

September 12 to 23, 1933.

"I'm still going strong on the Shannon Ranch and expect to be here yet for a few more days. Jim is a nice fellow to work for. About every other day he tells me to quit work early and go hunting jack rabbits up in the sage brush.

Last Sunday I was walking by a rubbish pile in the city dump while I was hunting and I found a suit of clothes. It's a full suit and in pretty fair condition. Like every good bum, I took the suit down to the ranch along with eight rabbits. I gave the suit a good wet wash and sewed on all the buttons for all were off. Homer found an old pair of riding pants and now I have four pair of pants.

On the evening of the 21st. Jim and I walked up to the grave yard and sat with our backs against a big vault and watched Reno bring forth its celebration for the campaign, "Buy in September and Save." The fireworks were rotten, so Jim amused me by pointing out in the dark, the spots where he knew the people who were buried there. An airplane tried stunting in a ray of light but Jim couldn't see well enough, so he started telling me about the people who were in the vault which we were using as a wind break.

Homer wanted me to cut his hair today, so I made a stab at it. He didn't have much, only a rim around which was about an inch and a half long. I tried some clippers and pulled most of it out. Once I said, "Well, it won't be long now." Homer said. "Yah, the way you're pulling it, it can't hold out much longer." I got some pretty deep dents in his hair and to cover them up I had to cut it short all over, so now his head is nearly clipped. Later he said his head was so bald that at night the millers fly against it and keep him awake. I suggested he use some black shoe polish on it.

It's getting cold nights now. I sleep with one blanket and four old overcoats on my bed, and wear one pair of white pants. The other day, while hunting, I found a good wool sweater up in the rubbish pile and now it is in my collection."

The riding pants Homer gave me fit right down in my boots good and the vest came with the suit, so I really felt dressed up when I was working.

September 24, 1933.

"Ernie came back the other night. He expected to work here and he's a little sore at me for getting his job. He told Jim that, "I would just as soon kill some *****as not then take the gas and end it." If he tries anything with me, he won't get gas but buckshot, for I keep the shotgun close by now.

I got my mail today. I heard from Glen. He expects to be on the go by the last of this month.

September 25 to Oct. 4, 1933.

"I'm doing a lot of tinkering around and we just got the reservoir dug and expect to cement it soon."

October 5 to 10th.

"Jim went to a prize fight last night. When he came home he woke me up at 12 o'clock and gave me a telegram he got in town. It was from Glen and said, "Come soon to New Lindsay Hotel Salt Lake."

I didn't know for sure what he meant. I thought he might be sick, so I got up and dressed and walked down to Sparks and at two o'clock I got on a freight train headed east. I was on a fruit train and got in an empty ice compartment in a reefer and went to sleep. When I crawled out of my hole in the morning I found myself out on the desert with sage brush and mountains all around. All day long the view was the same, towns were rare. Around Elko, Nevada we came across some ranches and good haying country. I had plenty of company on the train. Next car to me was an old bum of the road. He had a time table and ever so often he would take out a large magnifying glass to read it.

Late in the afternoon we stopped at a small division town, I went down town for something to eat, and then the city constable stopped me and made sure I got out of town on the train. At night I closed the trap door and had a warm room but the bed was terrible. There were wood slats with three iron slats upright cross ways and I had to lay on them. All night we rolled along and in the morning when the dawn was breaking I crawled out to find we were on the Great Salt Lake desert next to Salt Lake City. No vegetation of any sort was in sight. The desert was very flat with mountains in the distance. One mirage was sighted, a beautiful sparkling lake at the foot of a distant mountain. The sights on the desert are very deceiving. A horse in the distance may have a long neck like a giraffe. In places there were white thick water holes. The water would contain several kinds of minerals and those would crystallize around the edges and make a beautiful sparkling sight. From a distance the old water holes would look like sun shining on snow.

At last we came to the Great Salt Lake. I was on the Southern Pacific line and our train went to Ogden, thirty-six miles north of Salt Lake. The railroad company had built a rock dump about twenty miles long across the lake. The lake is sixty miles long and thirty miles wide. Each five pounds of water contains one pound of salt. My train slowed down to about ten miles an hour so I had plenty of time to look at the lake. The water was very blue and clear with patches of white salty foam on top. Around the edges of the dump the waves would beat against the rocks so that icicles were hanging to the rock. The lake is too salty for animal life and all I saw alive on it were two funny looking birds swimming around. The lake is slowly drying up and when we finally got across I saw men scooping up the salt with shovels along the old shores. We were then only a few miles out of Ogden but it took us three hours to get into the yards for the train slowed down to a walk.

Another lad from New Jersey and I bummed gardens as we went along to get something to eat. He went over the side first and came back with some rhubarb; then I went over and got some lettuce. Then we passed some onion pickers and they threw onions at us. I caught one so we had a vegetable breakfast. We came to one patch of what we thought were red ripe tomatoes. We both jumped off but when we got to the fence we found they were red peppers.

At last we got into Ogden. I went down town and got a dozen donuts for a dime and with my tramp clothes under one arm, I walked through town eating donuts. I hitchhiked down to Salt Lake City because the train service was rotten. I passed through a very fertile valley. It was mostly settled by Mormons, all irrigated, and there seemed to be an abundance of everything. Beautiful mountains were on one side with the trees turning to their autumn colors. At two o'clock I got to Salt Lake and in a few minutes I had found Glen in his hotel. Nothing was wrong; he just sent the telegram so I would come there after I finished my work at Reno.

He wanted to go prospecting and so did I. So, on the next day, Saturday, we visited every second hand store in town and started collecting our outfit. Every night we had to go to a show then have a pie afterwards.

On Sunday morning we were walking around the Mormon Tabernacle wondering what it was all about when we saw people going in. So, we thought we would go in and look around. We were probably the roughest looking sight in the building. Glen had no coat, just in shirt sleeves and no tie and I had on an old sweater, old rubbish pile pants and hob nailed shoes and a big hat in my hands.

Something was going to come off so we took a seat and waited. They pulled something off alright, for we had to sit there for three hours. They played a large pipe organ and sang for an hour. The tabernacle is noted for its sound effects. The inside is perfectly hollow like a long bowl upside down. Eleven thousand people were in it and many outside who could not get in. After the music, they had Mormon missionaries give talks on their work.

We had shipped out our camping outfit and Sunday night we expected to hop a freight train and go back to Reno, finish up my work for Mr. Shannon then go south to prospect.

At eleven o'clock at night after consuming an apple pie, we walked down to the Western Pacific railroad yards to catch our train. We found other bums who knew the getting on place and at one o'clock we boarded a merchandise train headed west. We rode on top the first forty miles and nearly got covered up by cinders. When the train stopped we went further back and found a flat car with a few tractors on and we rode that the rest of the night.

In the morning we got off at Carlin where we waited till eleven o'clock, then caught a Southern Pacific train headed to Reno. We opened up a box car and had a good place to sleep. Another lad with us bummed some sandwiches so I thought I would try it but the lady I asked would have me understand that she had all she could do to feed herself without feeding every bum that came along.

At eleven o'clock the next morning on Tuesday, we pulled into Sparks. We walked up to the Shannon Ranch and then I took Glen up to the jack rabbit patch for some shooting."

Mr. Shannon and Homer were glad to see us come back. We had dug out a place for a reservoir up by a small spring that came out in the creek just below his milking barn. He had a lean to shed where he fed cows but the milking parlor was out in the open. The cows were tame and at milking time all they had to do was walk up to a cow out in the open pen and sit down and milk.

Glen saw Homer getting his water for the kitchen out of the stream and just above the old cow had done her job right in the water. Glen didn't think too much of that. Mr. Shannon wanted a reservoir put in and a pipe run down to the kitchen so they had clean fresh water to use. That would be the only plumbing in the house.

October 11 to 21st.

"Glen is helping for his board. We had a terrible time to get forms for the reservoir then we lay around for a week before he could get a contractor to come up and put in the cement. On Sunday Glen and I took a hike up in the Peavine Mountains. We picked up ten parts of arrow heads on one ridge. In the mountains we killed a rattlesnake and picked up some ore around old shafts but it turned out to be only iron."

Just to keep busy while we waited for the cement man we hunted a lot of jack rabbits and kept the pig kettle full of good meat. Every so often an old truck would come for gravel and we would help load. Jim got from 50 cents to one dollar for each load, depending on the size of the truck and if we helped load. We covered Reno really well, went to 10 cent shows at night and never had it so good for a week.

October 22 to 28.

"A cement man and mixer came this week and put in the cement. Then Glen and I laid the pipe down in the house. We had a hell of a time at first. We're all packed up and ready to leave for the south, tomorrow on Sunday.

The pipe we laid was iron and all had to be cut, threaded and laid on a slope so the water would run out when Homer turned on the spigot. We made several trips into town to get everything to fit right but boy, were Homer and Jim ever happy when the water started running in their kitchen!!!

October 29, 1933. Sunday.

"We packed up this morning and were off for the south. We had pretty good luck hitchhiking and went 108 miles. We camped at Yenkersville. We are doing our own cooking and had rice and apple sauce."

While walking the road we had plenty of time to talk. Winter would be coming and we spent lots of time just figuring how we wanted to spend the winter and where. Several times we would leave the highway and go up on hills and just look for arrowheads. One such place we found at least 20 or 30 pieces of arrowheads but no really good ones. We carried full camping gear now; also each had a hard wool, war surplus blanket in our pack. Rations were the usual, dried fruit, oatmeal, raisins, pancake flour, small cans of condensed milk, sugar, salt and pepper, and usually hand dried bacon that keeps without refrigeration. Eggs were often bought at six to ten cents a dozen. We ate well and a lot of it at every meal. Cocoa was our main drink.

October 30, 1933.

"Got up early and it was rainy all morning. The first rain we had since May 5th. Nevada is mostly a desert. Got a ride through a mountain and caught a freight. We rode it for seventy-five miles through a hell of a sandstorm. It nearly blew us off the tracks. Got to Mina and the train wasn't going south until Thursday. We walked till dark and made camp in an old miner's mud house by a mine and we had a hot spring nearby. We heard a coyote howl in the night. The wind went down and it rained a little."

When we got on that freight we didn't know we were in for such a ride until it was too late. There were no empty boxcars or flat beds, so we rode on top of a car all afternoon. A terrible wind came up and that started the sandy desert to blowing. Before long we could hardly see from one end of the car to the other. We took our blankets out of our packs and wrapped them around our heads so we could breathe. The cars rocked and rolled, one hand held our blanket in place, the other one held on to the platform so we wouldn't blow off. When that train stopped we were sure glad to get off. We had sand in everything, from our hair to our boots. After waiting around for a while we found a breakie and he told us the train wouldn't leave until next Thursday.

After buying some supplies we got on the road heading south. Just at dusk we saw this mud house just off the road and by a creek. It was a one room house, mud walls, and dirt floor but it still had a good roof. We checked all over for rattlesnakes and made noise outside to scare anything away that might be in the sage brush. The mud walls were chunks of sod cut in pieces, piled on one another, maybe a foot or more thick, then plastered with mud. No door but we had a good place to get in out of the blowing sand.

October 31, 1933.

"When we woke up this morning the mountains around were covered with snow. After breakfast we stopped at the hot springs and washed our heads and cleaned up. Nearly all forenoon we hiked through a desert country, and then we hit a few mountains. Then we were lucky, a big car picked us up and took us to Tonopah. That is a silver camp and thousands of mines and diggings could be seen from the road. Tonopah was nothing but shacks with several thousand men waiting to go to work. Silver went up. Again we started hiking and just out of town we picked up a ride with another big car which took us to Goldfield. The country is all barren mountains with mines of all kinds on them. Goldfield was another old mining town which one time had a population of 50,000 people but now has about 1,000. It was all unpainted shacks ready to fall down. Two big hotels were the marks of a one-time booming town.

About two o'clock we left the city and started hiking south to Beatty with our next water about sixty miles onward. For three miles we climbed a mountain and came across some snow which had fallen the night before. Tonopah and Goldfield were both high up and very cold. We ate snow to save our water and after walking for six miles we had another streak of luck, for a man picked us up and hauled us to Beatty.

All the country was a desert and in places we could see our road stretch from 10 to 20 miles ahead of us from mountain to mountain. The sun had just fallen when we reached Beatty. It got dark very early so we made camp in a little grove by the Amagosa River. We could step across the Amagosa and it dried up a few hundred yards down further. Tonight was Halloween night but we didn't go out and play any jokes around here."

November 1, 1933.

"A cold night we had, the covers got mussed up and we shivered most of the night. After breakfast we packed up and walked into the little town. We had figured on outfitting here and prospecting in the mountains nearby. Beatty was another dead mining town. Like all small town gossips, the people wanted to know where we were from, what our business was and where we were going. It was a small place, nearly surrounded by mountains. On inquiring for burros we heard there were only about a half dozen left in the country and they were owned by the Indians. We talked to the old prospectors, one was now a barber. The other told us about the forty mile canyon and he wanted to join us and go in there for the winter and find placer gold. It gets cold around Beatty, so we gave up the idea of prospecting there.

In the middle of the afternoon we left Beatty headed west to look over the Sierra Nevadas. Our route took us across Death Valley and we were going to try and hitchhike across. We walked for five miles through barren mountain country to the ghost town of Ryalite. This old city was once a booming mining city with a population of about 15,000 people and now only three or four old shacks had a few prospectors in them. The entire city is in ruins. A big bank, the large store and other building have all fallen in. We picked up four old champagne bottles to carry water in along with our canteens. It is 35 miles across to Stove Pipe Wells Hotel where we can get water. We passed one house still in good shape made entirely of bottles. Late in the afternoon we left Ryalite and started walking across the Amagosa desert toward Death Valley. At sundown we stopped and cooked some rice and coffee, then after resting an hour we pushed onward across the desert. At nine o'clock we reached the foothills of the Amagosa Mountains and under an overhanging rock we made our camp for the night."

Glen carried his big post card size camera and a tripod along with a timing devise. We set the camera and then posed for the picture. We got a good picture of ourselves with all our packs on. The road crossing the desert was more like a sand trail. We could always tell where the road was but sand drifted back and forth often leaving soft sand to walk in. We didn't make very good time hiking across a desert.

November 2, 1933.

"After breakfast we again started walking. At the top of the Amagosa Mountains we came to Dry Light Spring where we took on more water and started a downward climb. All the country was barren rocky hills. At one in the afternoon we left the hills and looked out on Death Valley, stretching north and south. It was 16 miles to Stove Pipe and we could see what we thought was the hotel way out nearly on the other side of Death Valley.

We walked onward and soon the sun got hot as hell. We got a good sweat up and soon we began craving water. Our road was sandy and hard to walk in. We passed through several miles of mud rocky hills which looked as if it had been deposited by water. In places the earth was crusty and white with alkali, wind had blown the sand and dirt completely away from greasewood brush for they stood up with their roots 3 to 4 feet above the ground. Our water was running low and when we had six miles to go we had a pint left. We tried to save it, took only enough to wet our lips and mouth. Soon it was nearly all gone and we had 3 miles yet to go.

Our throats were so dry we couldn't swallow, our tongues swelled up and we could hardly talk as we pushed onward. Finally the sun went down and it cooled off a bit, and when we were less than a mile from town a car came along from Furnace Creek and took us to Stove Pipe.

There we found plenty of water and I drank nearly 2 quarts before I could stop. We made camp near Stove Pipe and after boiling some rice we lay down for a couple of hours. When we were lying down a coyote or gray fox came along, about 8 feet from me. It picked up a bacon rind and went off.

At nine o'clock we started walking so as to make the next watering place, which was supposed to be 35 miles on the next day. We had 6 quarts, 4 of which were in a gallon jug we had found. After walking a ways we started on the upgrade to get out of the valley. We walked till about one o'clock making about ten miles up the hill."

Walking across Death Valley is something we would never do again. We both agreed to that. We had no idea it would ever get that hot, besides carrying big packs on our backs. At first we could sweat but after we ran out of water we just dried up all over, our whole systems were out of water. At one place in the valley where two trails met there was a sign on a post. It made a spot of shade. Glen lay down with his head on that shade spot and at the time I had doubts if he would be able to get up. Of all the walking we had done, this was by far the worst.

November 3, 1933.

"Early in the morning we started walking. It soon began getting hot and our road was always uphill. This range of mountains was called the Paniment Mountains. We came to some water barrels but the water was oily. By noon we had only about a gallon of water left and we weren't to the top of the hill yet. We were fighting to save water by putting small stones in our mouth to keep it moist. At about one o'clock we came to some more water barrels. One had good water so we made a pipe out of paper and sucked it out of the bung hole. We drank a hell of a lot, filled our jug and again started on up the hill. Early in the afternoon we reached the top after 20 miles of uphill going.

As we started to go down the other side a highway man came along and picked us up. We rode to Lone Pine with him, all the country was hills and cliffs and canyons. That night we camped close to an outfit that was making a movie."

This was the second best ride we ever had, the first best being the last mile ride to Stove Pipe Wells. From Beatty we had walked across the Amagosa Desert, the Funeral Mountains, Death Valley and the Paniment Mountains. We figured probably 120 miles, maybe more, the way the trail curved around the sand dunes and hills. We could never walk in a straight line, especially when we were thirsty. Half way up the mountain coming out of the valley we started seeing wild burros. There were small herds scattered in the hills. They were all colors: spotted, striped and solid. All sizes too, from colts to old shaggy ones. These were the offspring of stock the old prospectors used years before.

Their grandparents were the ones the miners and prospectors used in the Gold Rush of 1850 and later.

In the old prospecting days of the gold rush a lot of the animals were just turned loose to make their own living. They ranged all through the foot hills of the mountains, cross breeding and in breeding to make every color there was. They could go a long time without water but they had to know somewhere in the hills where they could find water, even if it was alkali and unfit for human use.

The water barrels we found were to be used by cars or trucks that got hot climbing up the grade. They were a life saver for us. The barrel we drank out of had just a film of oil on the top. By putting a paper tube down through the film we could get oily tasting water but it sure did the trick for us.

November 4, 1933.

"Wind came up last night and nearly blew us away. We couldn't cook any breakfast so we finished the hot cakes we had cooked up in Death Valley, again we hit the highway headed south to look over the Kern River for placer mining and trapping. We walked nearly all day and in the evening caught a 60 mile ride south to where we turned west through Walker Pass. That night we made a dry and fireless camp behind some sand hills."

November 5, 1933. Sunday.

"For breakfast we didn't have much water to cook with so we made some hot cocoa. We cut out coffee because the night before last we drank a lot and couldn't sleep. We caught a ride through the pass and by lots of Yucca trees. We stopped at Kernville, right on the forks of the Kern River. We walked down stream and talked to some gold workers in the placer mines. When we were making camp we came across the best liar I have heard yet. He told us about how he could pick up big nuggets in Death Valley and how he could pan out a pound of gold a day in Mexico and how he put 20 pounds of gold in his crankcase to get it out of Mexico."

This was one of the best days we had for a long time. From Kernville we hiked down the road to a really small crossroad town called Isabella. It had one store and the post office was in one corner of that store. The old gent who ran it served as postmaster and storekeeper. He had most of the necessities to take care of the miners who were up and downstream. We followed a dirt or sand road downstream for several miles talking to placer miners along the way. The valley was filled with large cottonwood trees, willow and brush. It really looked like a nice place to spend the winter but no one was getting much gold. If they were, they weren't bragging about it too much. You couldn't blame them as no one wanted more miners to come into their territory.

November 6, 1933.

"The gold miners were hardly making wages so we left and hitch hiked down the Kern River to Bakersfield. There is placer gold all along the river bed but it is hard to get at. We made camp in a vacant lot."

November 7, 1933.

"We looked Bakersfield over but not too much to it. The big cotton strike was on there and there is some cotton picking around.

We took to the highway again, expecting to go to Needles, CA and look the Colorado River over for placer and we expected to winter there. We got one ride today and walked 30 miles. Just as we were going to make camp about five miles from Mojave, a freight train came along and stopped because of hot brakes. We boarded it and rode into Mojave and slept in a box car."

November 8, 1933.

"About seven in the morning our Santa Fe train came in and we boarded it and rode in a coal car across the Mojave Desert to Barstow, the next division. A freight train left there at one o'clock but when we boarded it a bull jumped on the car and put us off. Then we heard plenty of talk from other bums about the Santa Fe being a hard train on bums. That night at eight o'clock we sneaked up by the engine, had a breakie stop about three feet from us when we were hiding in the dark and we had to sneak back and when it started rolling we jumped on. It was cold as hell riding and we wrapped a blanket and a canvas around us to keep warm. We sat on top of a box car on an 18 inch platform, hollered, sang and whistled all night to keep from going to sleep. The train nearly stopped in front of the station and a husky bull saw us. He jumped on the car put his flash light on us and hollered, "What in hell is going on up here?" I said, "Oh, we're just pulling in." He said, "Well you sure as hell hit a hot place, get your stuff and get to hell off this train and get out of here." We piled off and then found a place where we got a few hours sleep."

November 9, 1933.

"After looking the town over and talking to a few prospectors we walked over to the Colorado River and gave it the once over. It was a large river, bigger than the Wisconsin and muddier than the Missouri. The river bottom was covered with soft wood trees but the mountains around were like a desert. We heard the gold was all flour gold and went for 3 or 4 cents to the yard. This meant we were in the wrong place again. In the afternoon we again took to the highway. Thought we would go north a ways on the Arizona side and look it over. After walking 15 miles and crossing the river we camped at Topock."

Needles was one of the hottest cities we were in on our travels. All dusty, sandy, dirty streets. We cooled off once by going in a restaurant and having a big dish of ice cream. The railroad bulls were tough. We heard stories how they often kicked a bum off a freight while it was on the go. It's hard enough to jump a freight on the go, grab something and climb on but to get off when a train is going very fast, you're in for a good roll every time.

November 10, 1933.

"We heard the country north wasn't any good, so we thought it over and decided we'd go to Phoenix or Tucson and try to start up a cheap café or eating joint. We got one ride through the desert country to Kingman and then we made camp in the ball park."

We had lots of time to talk over ideas as we walked. We had dozens of good and bad ideas of what to do, where to go and how to spend the winter. After being on Catalina Island and doing some cooking in the Home Dining Room I was willing to have our own business, if the price was right.

I had heard the story how two bums went into business and developed the famous five cent stew counters. Several years back these two hobos were following the carnivals trying to make a living by gambling. Their luck went rotten, so one day they found themselves broke. "Well partner," said one. "What we need is to start up our own business. You go hunting a big can, cut the top off and meet me out by the carnival field." They split up; one finding a five gallon can which he cut the top from. The other went down through the business section of town. He came to a grocery store, a bushel of potatoes were out on the walk on display. When the grocery man turned his back, several potatoes found their way into the bum's pockets. He passed several more stores, each time adding some vegetables: carrots, onions, any kind that were loose. Then he went to a butcher shop and said, "Say, mister, I just pulled into town with the carnival and I would like to get some old bones or soup meat for my dogs. I haven't any money on me now but I'll be in to buy more in the next few days."

The butcher, thinking he was lining up a good new customer was more than obliging. When the two bums met, a new business was born. They started the fire, filled the can up with water, added the bones, meat and vegetables and in two hours were calling, "Right this way folks, get a large can of the best jungle stew in the world for only five cents."

November 11, 1933.

"Today was Armistice Day and lots of people were celebrating. We split up for we thought we could hitchhike easier. I started out ahead and I walked all day without a ride. I walked 28 miles to Hackbury and built a fire and was cooking hot cakes for supper when Glen walked in and joined me. Glen had a cold settle in his ear so we took a cabin for the night."

I believe hitchhiking in this area was about the toughest we had found. Glen had walked all day too.

When we hiked that far, the packs get pretty heavy. One ear was bothering him badly so we decided to sleep indoors instead of on the ground.

November 12, 1933. Sunday.

"We said to hell with hitchhiking so we flagged down a bus and rode to Ashfork. There we paid for a fare on a freight train and rode in the caboose to Prescott where we took a hotel for the night."

This was a first for us, to buy a ride on a freight train. The caboose was nice to ride in and the conductor was talkative and he seemed to enjoy company. Mostly sage brush, desert and rock besides having all the good cold water we wanted to drink.

November 13, 1933.

"I hitchhiked to Phoenix and Glen took a bus there because of his ear. He got there first and left a note on a stick of chewing gum by the outer steps of the post office, so I could find him. He had to go to a doctor with his ear. We looked all over town for a restaurant site but none appealed to us, besides the city seemed awfully dead."

November 14, 1933.

"After looking around town some more we decided to go to Tucson and look around. Glen had to wait all day for some pictures, so I started hitchhiking. It was desert all the way and I got in early in the evening. I got a 50 cent hotel room, looked around some then went to a show."

November 15-16, 1933.

"We tinkered around town, went to more shows, read a little at the library. In the night we were awakened by a woman screaming. I guess she was dreaming and thought she saw a white cat in her room. She was afraid to open the door or put on the light and she screamed for five to ten minutes and no one could get in to help her."

That was some night to remember. Most everyone in the hotel was awakened. All running up and down the hall, half dressed, wondering what was going on. Some pounded on her door; they could hear her scream about a white cat. After things quieted down we finally finished our night's sleep.

Fifty cents per night was the top rate we ever paid for a hotel room and we always made good use of it. There would be a community bathroom down the hall, everyone used it, took turns, often a lineup of customers each morning waiting his or her turn. If we were lying over for a day we used the bath tub to wash some clothes.

November 17, 1933.

"We decided to head for the west today. We met a bunch of kid gamblers down at the railroad tracks. They got twenty dollars from one kid but the cops got them. Some clever fellows worked Glen for 35 cents and they jumped me but I wouldn't bite. We got a train out at night and rode in a gondola all night."

That afternoon we spent our time down by the railroad yards, out in the hobo jungle. This was a real jungle, seemed more like a park. Nice trails were zig zagging through the brush, some large cottonwoods were scattered along a small creek. Bums were all over, some just resting for a day or so, others were waiting for freighters to go out. Both directions, some were heading east, others west. A few camp fires were burning, cooking up whatever they had scrounged up in town. That night the only empty car we could find was an empty gondola car. One they use for coal or ore. When we climbed in the car and sat down along the side we found plenty of company. The car was well filled up on both sides, 40 and 50 men off the road. Some had been in the gondola when the train came in and they talked about the east while those of us who just got on talked of what we would do in the west. One young man said he was a prize fighter and he was going west to line up some fights.

November 18, 1933.

"At six o'clock in the morning we got to Yuma, CA. Just after we left there about seven o'clock, Glen had another fainting spell.

He was out for about ten minutes. Bloody mucus came from his mouth; he jerked his arms, head and jaw. He closed his jaw very tight and bit up his tongue. We rode all day and Glen felt pretty good. There were fifty of us in the gondola and we came near Los Angeles. Some of them jumped off, afraid of the cops, twelve miles out of town. About twenty of us rode in and two bulls jumped the car when we were a few miles out. When the train stopped they called the police wagon and gave us a free ride to the jail. We checked in all our belongings and they gave us a number then took our description and then we were put in the cooler. There were about forty of us altogether. My number was 33633. The beds were three decks high and made of steel. The place was as cold as hell, no heat of any kind. We shivered around till eleven o'clock and then we were given three blankets apiece. There was another cooler across the hall where they threw the drunkards. It seemed to be a big night for them for there were 40 or 50 in there. Some were out cold while others hollered all night and we couldn't sleep."

It had been a long day for us. Riding all night and trying to catch some sleep while sitting alongside a steel gondola. Freight trains aren't smooth riding by any means. We felt every bump and the cars were continuously swaying back and forth. Then Glen getting the epilepsy fit which scared many of the hobos half to death. Most of them thought he was going to die right in their traveling car. Several darkeys were sure the end was coming; they really started praying to the good lord not to strike down any of their comrades in their car. By the late afternoon, Glen felt a lot better but he had an awful sore tongue.

The last time we rode into Los Angeles we had jumped off way out beyond the city limits because we had heard about tough railroad cops. This time we thought being in a gondola and out of sight that we could ride in and get off just before the train stopped. Besides, it was getting dark and our chances were better. We were wrong for when the train slowed up two tough railroad cops climbed up the ladder of the gondola and put their flashlights on us. They were well armed, a billy club and a gun hung on each one's side. The train seemed to take forever to crawl the last few miles into the yards where several truck type paddy wagons were waiting to escort us to the jail.

November 19, 1933. Sunday.

"At an ungodly hour, about 4:30 this morning we were aroused from behind the bars and marched out to breakfast. The only manners shown were when we took off our hats to sit; we were given a big spoon and a plate of some kind of mush over some kind of meat loaf and two slices of bread. We also had coffee with no sugar or milk and it tasted so rotten I couldn't drink it. I thought probably they saved the bath water from prisoners to make it.

We were all still hungry when we left the table and went back to our cells. Most of us lay down to finish our sleep when the trustee came in and took our blankets. We shivered till the sun came up. We had nothing to do except think. Those who smoke and who were out of tobacco were in a hell of a fix. The men who had the tobacco smoked first, then the others. All yelled for the butt and the butt would go to four of five fellows. Finally noon came, we marched out and had beans and plain bread and the same coffee. We got some more bread, I ate seven slices but we didn't get enough beans.

In the afternoon we lay around and sang, slept or just thought. We heard our trial would be that night. Toward evening more fellows were put in our lock up. For supper I fared better, I got a plate and a half of beans and I got eleven slices of bread. At eight o'clock we were all lined up in the hall and a lawyer asked us all how we felt or how we pleaded, guilty or not guilty. When he called "Kussmaul, Glen how do you feel?" Glen hollered, "All right." We all plead guilty and were taken in a group before the lady judge. She just asked where we were going and then sentenced us to one day for evading railroad fare. We were to get out at six o'clock the next morning. That night we all had to take a bath and we were sent upstairs and I had to sleep on the floor with a lot of other prisoners."

Sunday was a day to remember and it seemed to last longer than two ordinary days. We tried to rest some, but lying on a steel bunk, we tossed and turned all the time. The noise was terrible, with forty or more fellow prisoners, there would be a lot of cussing, singing, whistling, and bragging among the mixture of inmates. There were old time hobos who were used to getting a bath and these free meals, plus darkeys, Mexicans, kids, and men of all ages.

One old darkey amused the fellows when one man asked him what he was in for. He said, "I's in for borrowing money." One of the young men piped up and said, "They can't put you in jail for borrowing money." The darkey said, "Well, I is here ain't I?" The young fellow said, "They can't do that legally." The darkey said, "Well, it was this way. I had to hit the gentleman over the head with a club before he would lend me his money."

Another darkey told about riding a freight train into Tucson. He was in a box car when the train was switching around in the yards. He said he opened the door to see where he was at and saw a figure in the dark. Thinking it was another bum he hollered out, "Hey boss, is this too soon?" The other guy was a railroad dick and he said. "No, you black cuss, you're just in time, pile off that train."

The only reading material in our cell was two pages from some newspaper. When I got my hands on it I believe I read every word forward and backwards. It wouldn't have been so bad spending time if they had a library available. We were entertained royally in the afternoon by one really old colored gent. He must have been well into his seventies, probably five and a half feet tall, not real thin or fat, grey hair and beard which had not been cut for months. He had long arms that came way down to his knees. Old greasy looking pants, patched up shirt and an old black jacket. He was a preacher by profession or so he said. But he was true to his religion because he preached to all of us for more than an hour. Everyone seemed to enjoy listening; it was different from what we had been hearing all day long.

Part of his sermon went like this: "We can compare our religion like a possum. Once there was a possum up a tree and they shaked him and one foot come a loose, then they shaked him and shaked him and two foot come a loose, and they shaked him and shaked him and three foot come a loose and they shaked him and shaked him and four foot come a loose, then low and behold his tail was wrapped around a limb and all hell couldn't shake him a loose. Now, that is the way with our religion, when it once gets in you all hell can't pull you a loose."

One old timer of the road went into great detail on how he could always bum something to eat. First thing he did was look the alleys over and find himself a half starved kitten. Then he'd go up to a house, knock on the door and when the Mrs arrives say, "Madam, will you please give me some salt? A lady down the street gave me this here cat to cook up but she didn't have any salt." He said he traded many an alley cat for good grub.

You can believe what you want from all the stories you hear from the fellows on the road. At least they're entertaining to listen to and it helped pass the time away.

I even got so that I enjoyed the meals. The last supper was the best; great big lima beans mixed in some kind of goulash. Lots of beans and from then on lima beans were my favorite.

When it came to taking baths we were all put in a large room where we had chairs or benches to sit on and undress. They called us by name and Glen was called first, there were eight or ten showers, soap and a towel and each took his turn. We were careful to undress in a corner because we both had on our money belts. When Glen's turn came I watched his clothes. After a while Glen had his bath or shower and I was waiting and they called Glen's name again. We had quite a time with the trustee proving to him that Glen had his and they had his name down twice instead of me. I finally got my shower. We needed it and that was one of the highlights of our stay.

November 20, 1933. Monday.

"At 4:30 in the morning we were again rousted out for breakfast. This time we had oatmeal mush over the meatloaf. It was alright with me because I knew we would soon be out and I could get some real grub. At 6:30, just as it was getting light, we got our baggage and were turned out. The air smelled pretty good again. Glen and I walked downtown and took a hotel room then we went out and got a real feed. I hunted up Mr. Johnson, my old friend, the painter, and we all took in a rotten show at night."

When we left the jail in the morning one of the jailers escorted us to the front door and said, "Come back again, men."

After we checked into our usual 50 cent room hotel we went right downtown to the Chinese restaurant that served a four course meal for ten cents.

We talked over how we would spend the winter and decided that the Kern River looked to be the best place to find placer mining, hunting and trapping. We wrote home and told the folks what we would be doing and had them send our thirty-two special rifle and some traps, also some extra clothes and small items, all sent parcel post to Isabella, general delivery.

November 21, 1933.

"We went shopping today, after visiting every second hand store in town we finally bought a tent for $6.50 and some other trash. I called up Ernie Arnold but he was busy so we took in some more shows. Some of the trash we bought included two large heavy blankets. These blankets were square, supposed to be used when furniture is packed for moving. They were long enough and real heavy, just right for our needs. We also bought a single shot twenty-two rifle, two metal gold pans, shovel, small axe and other useful items. All were used merchandise and didn't cost us too much.

November 22, 1933.

"We went to all the second hand book stores and came away with a small library for our future home on the Kern River. Ernest came around in the evening with his car and drove us around a bit. We went out to Hollywood. They have everything well lit up there. We were down by the Coliseum where the Olympics were held in 1932."

November 23, 1933.

"We said goodbye to our friends and started hitchhiking up to Bakersfield. We had split up but we both caught a ride right through. I got in first, took a hotel, then went down by the post office steps and left a note with my address in a stick of gum by the steps. Glen soon found it and came to my hotel. The country coming up was mostly a desert and mountains with a very winding road."

November 24, 1933.

"We went to the express office and had our goods shipped here from Reno, but we have to wait here a couple of days for them to arrive. The city is filled with cotton pickers, lots of darkeys and Japs.

November 25, 1933.

"We did more shopping today and bought a small stove and a lot of grub."

November 26, 1933.

"We blew ourselves to a couple shows today. Saw Will Rogers in "Dr. Bull."

November 27, 1933.

"We shipped our goods by the stage up to Isabella and we hitchhiked up. We got a ride in a truck up the river and got here about three o'clock. We walked down stream to where we camped before and found the two miners still at work. They were making pretty good some days. We went back to Isabella and an old gent told us of a barn with hay in where we could sleep and we put in a good night."

November 28, 1933.

"Early in the morning we went back downstream and found a place for our tent, right below an overhanging rock and trees around for a wind break. We had a man haul our luggage down and by noon we were at work making a place for our tent. Just as we started to work a little snow storm passed over. After much work and cussing we finally got our tent up and bed made by dark. We used our little stove outside and candles for light because our gas lantern wouldn't function properly."

November 29, 1933.

"We were up early and at work getting things in shape. We got our stove in and built some benches. We have a great place for our camp. It is close to the river and we have a good view up and down and of the surrounding mountains."

The Greenhorn Mountain range ran all along just to the back of us. We could walk maybe a block and then start up the mountain. Sage brush flats were all along the river next to the mountain but the mountain itself was well covered with pine trees, large and small; patches of brush were scattered throughout. Rocks all over, the whole valley was covered with round, smooth rocks, laid down by rivers of the past. Large cottonwood trees lined the river banks. Willow brush would hide the river in places. It is called the Kern River but really it's nothing but a big overgrown creek. We could jump from rock to rock and cross it most any place we wanted to.

Years back there had been lots of activity on this river and up most every ravine or valley leading to the river. Old camp sites or wood buildings that had wasted away were scattered up the valley. We raided those places for all the lumber we needed to make our beds, wash stand, and other needs. We had a bow saw for getting wood and we had brought nails with us. We cut a big hole in the side of the tent, lined it with tin, and then put the stove chimney out a ways then up to get the draft. The overhanging rock made a perfect dry storage place to keep wood or other merchandise.

Our sheet iron stove was really a good one, better than we expected

as we found as the days went by. The door was down in front, a nice size oven was next to the fireplace, leaving the top with all the space we needed to cook. We had a damper in the chimney, just a little wood made a good fire to heat up the tent. The tent was eight by twelve, stove in the back end, bunks down both sides, no room for a table, we nailed six inch boards on the sides of our bunks to sit and eat on. The bunk was filled up with pine boughs, then the canvas and then our blankets. Really cozy, best set up we had had for a long time.

November 30, 1933.

Thanksgiving Day. "We're still getting things straightened out. We made another cupboard for our library which is composed of 29 volumes from Shakespeare to a cookbook which we had picked up in a second hand stores. We worked till noon and when we thought about dinner, we decided to let it go and have an early supper. Glen was uptown and got some more grub and some gas for the lantern, but still the lantern wouldn't work. We have a good notion to see how far we can throw it."

We were probably about three miles by the road from Isabella. By following a trail by the river then cutting across some hills, we could shorten the distance by maybe a mile. There was a kind of a dirt road above our camp; it followed the mountain around and went several miles downstream to two ghost towns, Keyesville and Budfish. (Budfish is not named on the California ghost town list on the Internet; it might be misspelled or may never have been incorporated. There is no Bullfish either.) They were probably five or six miles downstream. Just a very few miners were living there trying to make a living placer mining. Maybe once a day or once every two days some old car or truck would use the highway. When a car did go by we would always look up and give them a wave of our hand. As time passed, these folks acted like good neighbors, some would stop in, visit a while, often asked if we wanted a ride to town or if we needed anything from the store.

December 1, 1933.

"One of the miners let us have a sluice box and we picked out a spot and started mining today. The first pail full of dirt showed two colors so we kept on. We worked like hell and got some fine stuff. In the afternoon I got the gas light fixed, and then I went up stream and snagged a big sucker fish. We mined till late and came away with about seventy-eight cents worth of gold to pay us for our day's work. After every pail of dirt we would look the bottom over for a long time and if we saw a piece of gold, we would pick it out with tweezers and put it in a bottle. In the evening we tried out the oven. I baked some pretty good biscuits and Glen made some corn bread."

Our first day of placer mining was more like a learning experience or schooling. We were lucky to have a good sluice box given to us. It's important to have a good one so as to save any gold that goes through. The box was about twelve inches wide by six feet long, just two sides about six inches high and open on both ends making a trough. The first three feet have half inch high slats nailed across, about two inches apart, then it had a mesh screen with a piece of burlap or any thick wool cloth under that. This screen is held by slats on the side so it can be taken out and washed in a gold pan. The sluice box is placed in the current on a slant so water runs through it fast. Usually we laid it in the edge of the stream then made a rock dam out a ways to force the fast current down through it. Then we would get a bucket of dirt and pour it in at the top. The fast water washes down through the trough, taking most of the rock and mud through it. Bigger rocks are usually removed by hand. Gold is heavy, as soon as it hits the water it goes right to the bottom. Bigger pieces settle in the first slats, fine gold will settle in the screen below and stay in the burlap. After we dumped pail after pail of gravel in the sluice box, we always were looking in the first ripples or slats to see if any large pieces showed up. Then we would take the box out of the stream, take off the screen and wash out the burlap in our gold pan. Iron particles, really black in color, always lodged in the burlap too. We would have maybe a cupful of what we called "mud" in our pan. We would then gently swirl the pan in water, always at an angle so the mud would wash out. After several minutes we would have just the gold left in the bottom of the pan. It's really yellow and stood right out. Often we would find just specks of "flour gold", fine as dust, still usable but not enough to try and save. If we did find a place that had a lot of flour gold and it was worth saving, we would put a drop of mercury in our pan. Mercury adheres to gold and with a few swirls of the pan would soon pick up all the fine gold. Mercury is really heavy and was the last thing to stay in our pan. We would use the same mercury over and over until a lot of gold dust is trapped in it. Then to get the two separated, we would put the mercury in our gold pan, put a slice of potato on top and put our pan over the stove and heat it up really well. When the mercury gets so hot it evaporates into the potato, leaving pure fine flour gold in our pan.

December 2, 1933.

"We were up at six and had breakfast of cream of wheat and corn bread and then went to work. We found a little more color in our buckets than yesterday. We worked several places but nothing would pay out. In the afternoon we were tired of working for nothing so we rigged up a fish line and took the gun and went out and spent most of the afternoon. We got one squirrel in a trap but we saw a hundred more. We got one fish and I snagged it. We have about twenty cents worth of gold now. These first two days have been hard on our eyes trying to see gold in the bottom of our sluice box. Our meals consist mostly of beans, spuds, dried fruit, with corn bread and syrup for dessert.

The squirrel we got is called a ground squirrel. They look just about like our gray squirrels back in Wisconsin. Only these have a shorter tails and they live only in the ground. They burrow in, make dens just like prairie dogs only these are true squirrels.

They headed for their dens just as soon as they saw us. If we shot one it would be gone down in the den anyway and we would lose him. So, Glen set some traps and from then on we trapped a lot of squirrels. They were very good eating, although one rancher we talked to said they were poison, but we had already been eating them for some time and we didn't believe him.

We're finding fish quite plentiful. Mostly all suckers but we are eating them quite often. Small valley quail are scattered up and down the valleys in the brush areas. We pick them off with the twenty-two rifle. Two make a good meal for us. Half way to town is one of our really good neighbors. He goes by the name of Dad Wilson. He is tall and lean, in his seventies, always dressed in high leather boots, regular boot pants, old shirt and a ten gallon hat. He's a really old prospector, ex-moonshiner, and cowboy. He is really sociable; we always stop and visit when we go by. He gave us a lot of good pointers on mining, and a jar with sourdough starter, so from now on we can have sourdough bread and pan bread. Dad Wilson lives in a tent, has an extra lean-to for cooking along with a small table and a chair. He came into this area several years back for his health. He finds this climate is the best for his asthma. He would often walk down to our camp just for a little visit.

December 3 and onward

"We have lost all track of dates now but I guess it's somewhere near the eighth or ninth of December. The days go so fast and it's all we can do to keep track of the months. We have been hunting gold now for more than a week and now we have about 60 cents worth of the precious stuff. We were working below camp on a rocky flat but the nuggets we got there could hardly be found when they were placed for safe keeping in a bottle. The bottle is a very small one but still it's many times too large for our yellow wealth. For the last few days we have been prospecting upstream. Today we dug in an old hole and found good color, so we moved our sluice box up there. It's about a mile and a half upstream so the walk to and from work will be worth all the gold we get without counting the work of digging it out from beneath three to four feet of boulders and sand.

We found out this afternoon we had been making a bad mistake. Our watches were one hour and twelve minutes slow, we had even written home and told them that it was getting dark here at 3:30. Also, we thought we were doing pretty good to get up at six in the morning and be at work by seven thirty.

The last few days we would usually lay off the gold in the afternoon and go fishing or hunting ground squirrels. We snagged some big suckers and have our eyes on some big white fish. The ground squirrels are hard to get. There are plenty of them but they are smart.

Tonight I washed up the dishes for a change. It's the second time since we made camp. If we looked hard, or maybe not so awfully hard, we could see what we had on our plate for the last week. Our clothes are doing a little better. We have some brown shirts which don't show the dirt. We have worn them for the last six weeks and they don't need washing yet.

Glen told me this morning that last night he did something that is very seldom done. I asked, "What's that?" And he said. "I cut my toenails without taking my socks off." As far as washing goes, we haven't enough socks left to wash.

We're getting to be awfully big eaters. Usually for supper we each eat a squirrel or a big fish, then a quart or more of beans and then have another quart of dried fruit or have a slab of corn bread. That's big enough for an ordinary man for a week.

I haven't shaved now since we made camp. Pretty soon I will have to comb it before eating so the gravel won't fall on my plate. Our whole floor was nothing but sand until the other day when I found some old boards a mile upstream and now we have a part wood floor. The sandy floor was the best in a way. All we had to do with any dirt or refuse was to throw it on the floor and kick sand over it. Then when the floor got too polluted, we would carry it out with a shovel and bring in a new clean shovelful."

We probably had the best camp in the valley, maybe not the neatest, but we had everything handy. We were close to the stream, out of the wind, always had dry firewood, even had a nice one hole toilet built over in the brush. Our plates and pans were aluminum. It got to be a regular chore, every few days, maybe once a week; we took all utensils down to the creek and scrubbed them with sand. They would really shine when we finished that job. Wood was easy to get, pine cones were plentiful and the cones made a quick hot fire. One of us found a big cow skull with long horns and we posted it on one of the corner posts that held up the tent.

Different miners were always coming or going, looking the stream over, and trying to find a new place to placer. Some would camp close by for a day or two then move on. The whole valley had been heavily worked during the gold rush days. Heavy dredges had torn up the stream bed and the banks, tailing piles were strewn around all over. Only in places where the river ran through solid rock crevices or where the boulders were too big and heavy would there be places where the dredges missed. French Gulch was maybe a half mile above us. It ran up a side valley and the old timers said over a million dollars in gold was taken out of that valley alone. Then the Chinese came through and they worked and combed the area where the dredges missed. I often found old Chinese shoes that were left in the rocks. Dad Wilson told us about a tunnel the Chinese dug just below his place. He said they dug a hole down to the bedrock and then tunneled along the rock, scraping up the loose dirt off of bedrock and washing out the gold. The tunnel caved in on several workers, and from the story he heard, the rest closed up the hole and the Chinese men are still buried there.

Someone built a large stone house up French Gulch. The walls look to be two feet thick, it has windows and two doors and still in pretty good shape. When it is vacant, whoever wants to can move in. A small stream runs close by, so water is available. A tough looking red headed man by the name of Young moved in sometime in the winter. He had his wife with him and he placer mined up French Gulch. We called him Red and he was kind of an odd sort of fellow and his wife wasn't much different. She had the appearance of being a cross between a Mexican and an Indian.

All of us used the water from the river for drinking and cooking. No one had heard of pollution in those days. The river originated way up in the mountains above Kernville.

December 16, and backwards.

"We had quite a surprise the other day when we got a letter from our brother Rud, whom we thought was at home but was in Los Angeles. We soon heard from home and they explained matters. Rud had just bought a good car and a few days after, he and three others got drunk and Rud drove it home and wrecked it on Parsley Hill.

Day before yesterday after dark here came Rud and Gennings Bilderman into camp with twenty pounds of beans and ten pounds of prunes. They are looking for a dairy job or any kind of work and just came up to see us. It was raining most of the time they were here but when it cleared up yesterday, I took them up to our mining hole a mile or more up the creek and told them they could start work. It was a big hole and filled with water. They sat around and worked around it for twenty minutes. Then they thought they would bail it out and find some gold. By the time they got the water bailed out they nearly had their fill of mining. They picked up lots of mica and thought it was gold.

They left today, back for Los Angeles. Three of them slept in our bunks and I slept on the floor. When they once got in bed they couldn't move till morning.

It rained here for four days straight, cleared up here last night and is a little colder now. All the mountains are covered with snow and the winds sweeping down from them makes an ice box of the valley.

Tex moved today, or rather pulled out for the mother lode country up north. He gave us his two sluice boxes. The Petersons also moved. He is going to work for the government on a road at Keysville about two miles down.

We did a little mining today. We took out twenty cents worth. A man came along and told us the land we were on was owned by Old Frank and he wanted to lease it. The place wasn't much good to mine so we finished up our hole and moved out."

It was quite a reunion we had in the mountains, having we three brothers and Gennings here. We had plenty of grub and our visitors did a good job of eating. When they left we packed them up with dried fruit, pan bread, and enough of necessities to get by on for a while. When we heard again from home later, they were both back home. They rode the freights out and back and nearly froze going home. Bumming freights back to Wisconsin in the heart of winter is no easy chore.

We moved our sluice boxes back down stream right close to our camp. We dug down through rock and gravel from three to four feet and found good color on top of the bed rock. Our work hole is about six feet from the stream. Water fills the hole every night and after we bail that out we dig down to just the top of bedrock. Gold goes right to the bottom. When we get close to bedrock we save all the muck, put it in five gallon pails, then carry it over and wash it through the sluice box. When we came to the bedrock, which is usually rotten granite, we scrape the rock with a large spoon, save all the scrapings because that is where the gold lays. When we found a crevice in the rock we had bent irons to dig them out, or we used a bar to break the rock making the crevice large enough so we could clean it good. Usually these scrapings would go only into our gold pans and we washed the gold out by the swirling motion. It was always more fun to pan the mud, get down to the very last ripples in the pan and see the yellow gold come to light.

Many a morning we counted the five gallon buckets of water we had to throw out of our work hole before getting down to the bottom. Five hundred buckets would be the usual amount, more or less, depending on how deep and wide the hole was. This was really good exercise for our backs and other muscles.

December 26, 1933.

"About a week ago we borrowed some traps from a man who went away last summer and never came back. We're trying to get a few furs. If it pays out then we will buy a license. The other day Glen caught a wildcat; we're going to have the hide tanned and send it home.

We have been all over the mountains and on the top looking for trapping trails. There are high rugged mountains, the Big Horns in the back. These are the Green Horns by our camp. There are lots of deer tracks up in the hills and one spot we saw where bears had been digging the roots of some kind of brush.

Gold mining is slow. We both caught colds so we laid off work. We celebrated Christmas in grand style. We started eating and making candy the day before Christmas and we had plenty of fudge. I made a pudding and for dinner we had cornbread and honey, pudding and candy. Then for supper we had mashed potatoes, gravy, squirrel, cornbread, pudding and candy again.

We have been doing lots of fishing lately. We catch them and store them in an old prospect hole for future use. We caught seven big suckers today. The ground squirrels are still too smart for us. We have tried every way to trap them but so far have only caught a few.

I cleaned up the bed today and made it over. A little of all kinds of junk was in it. The other day Glen sat on my hat. He took and held it over his socks and said. "This ought to soon straighten it out." The night before Christmas a mole came in the tent and raised a mound all around; when Glen saw it he began to sing his Christmas carols and said. "It was the night before Christmas, when down in his hole, the creature that was stirring was a darn little mole."

Every few days we go up to Isabella for some groceries and mail. Usually every week or so, we have a letter from Mother at home. In her Christmas letter she sent a five dollar bill for our

Christmas present. This was a lot of money to us, more than we made so far panning for gold. Once a week at least, when we were in town, we would splurge and each have a five cent candy bar. They were full four ounce bars, either a Power House or Mr. Goodbar. That candy bar would last us a long way on our walk back to camp, taking a small bite after so many steps.

We always wrote home at least every two weeks. The folks were always worrying about us, afraid something would happen, especially if Glen would get a really bad epilepsy fit and be all alone somewhere. Glen and I never worried about that and I don't believe he had an attack all winter.

We always passed Dad Wilson's camp and usually sat and chatted a while. We told him about being way back in the Big Horns and he told us to always have our big rifle along as there could be a few mountain lions left there. He told about one prospector who went back in there and all anyone found of him was his leather boots with his feet still in them. That was several years back but at least it put us on guard.

January 7, 1934. Monday.

"We celebrated New Years by having more candy and also a pie made by putting chocolate tapioca pudding in a pie shell. Mr. Dad Wilson is coming back to his camp. He got Ptomaine poisoning from fried spuds on a tin plate. We pulled the traps up and took them back and today he lent us six of them.

Last Saturday Glen and I took the two rifles and went back into the mountains. We crossed the Green Mountains and saw where lots of mining work had been done. We came out on a big valley between the Green and Big Horns. That country is filled with big sugar pine and mountain mahogany. The sugar pine is a very sturdy tree; some are five to six feet in diameter, rearing up their great trunks seventy to one hundred feet and then tapering off quickly. The mountain mahogany is a bushy tree, more of a bush which has a very red bark and small leaves. Deer and cattle feed on it.

We saw some mountain squirrels. They're twice as big as a fox squirrel and have a beautiful silver colored fur. We circled about and when we were coming through some brush on top of a mountain a deer jumped out. Glen got one shot at it as it disappeared around the hill and it kept going. About a mile further on, another deer jumped up from a clump of brush. I shot with the small rifle but missed and Glen emptied the thirty-two of five shells and still the deer kept going, untouched.

I'm mining down below where we first started. I dug out a crack and got some good color, so I have kept digging. One day I made about a dollar or less and today I took out about two bits. We mined from Thanksgiving till New Years and all the gold we got we sent home for a souvenir.

We have plenty of visitors around now. Two fellows moved into the tin shack above here. One, Joe, is a lawyer from Chicago. The other, Warren, is a roustabout prospector. They don't get along very well now and are liable to split up most any time.

Today I met four more men, two who moved into a tent above us. I was talking to one of the older men and he said that they were oil drillers. His sidekick was an oil refiner and he was an oil tool machinist. They said that Hoover had put them all on the bum."

This Saturday we went back into the mountains. Each one of us carried a packsack on our back; we always carried a small pick, shovel, a few other tools and our lunch. Lunch would be cornbread and beans. In one valley we took our samples of dirt after digging down. Those we put in small bags and packed them back to camp where we put each sample in our gold pans and washed it out. One sample showed a nice sized nugget, maybe a little bigger than a match head, but we never got back to that valley where we took the sample; it was too far back, a dry valley, and so no water to work with. We always used a compass to go by as a person could get lost that far from camp.

Glen had a few traps sent from home and with the other six we borrowed; Glen has quite a trap line out. He runs the trap line each forenoon while I keep mining. We have several wild cat furs, some skunk, once in a while and a nice jack rabbit, which are very good eating and a big meal. We do get quite a few cottontail rabbits in the valleys with the twenty-two rifle.

Joe Garrity, the lawyer from Chicago is quite a city dude. We could tell he was used to having plenty of money from the way he dressed. Really nice, highly priced leather boots, good boot pants, nice shirts, always had a long ivory cigarette holder in his mouth and smoked store bought cigarettes. Joe has friends in Los Angeles and they brought him up here to hide out for a while. About every two weeks after he came here, a car would pull in and bring him fresh supplies. We could tell by his hands and fingernails that he had never done any hard work in his life. When he walked around he always carried a nice cane in one hand and a nice twenty-two rifle in the other. Joe told me later on that his job was to lease entire large buildings in Chicago, and then he would sublease them out. The depression wiped him out.

The oilmen are across the creek from us and up a ways. They have a really nice tent, plenty of supplies and some mining tools. A big car brought them up from Los Angeles, unloaded all their gear and then left. In the days ahead that car would come back ever so often, bring supplies, stay a while and then leave. On one trip a young lady was along, the daughter of the older gent. They have a shotgun and have been getting some jack rabbits and quail for meat. We often gave them fish as we keep stocked up pretty good.

January 10, 1934.

"We were up to see the newcomers the other night. Both men are comical old jiggers, and said they were kind of scouting around and looking for the men who voted for Hoover. They caught on to Warren. One said that their first morning there, Warren come over and said, just to be neighborly he would take them down below and show them where they could get some pretty good gold. One went down with him, they said, just to be polite, and made Warren think he knew a little something. He dug around for a couple of hours even though he knew there was nothing there.

Glen and I went up to Kernville today. The Big Blue Mine might be opening up and jobs could be had. The Big Blue had run for years, took out lots of gold but the main vein they were following was petering out, besides water seepage was a problem.

By cutting each other's hair, word spread around that I could barber. From then on I could be working a placer mine and along would come a prospector with a pair of scissors and a comb and wanted his hair cut. I would stop work, have the fellow sit on a big rock and go to cutting his hair. I must have given two dozen or more haircuts from that time until spring. All had the same style, short and ragged and all at no charge.

One miner who lived up in the valley showed us some really good pieces of "float" he had picked up. Float is a piece of rock that has either a small streak of gold or small nuggets showing. Usually always found in quartz rock. We spent quite a few hours looking up dry creek beds, picking up one rock after another but we never did find any. Float rocks could be crushed and the gold extracted by using mercury. Float originally came from a quartz vein that was part of a mountain at one time. Earthquakes and floods broke up the mountain and these pieces were scattered down in the valleys. The free gold we get by placer mining all originated the same way; only floods and time have ground up the rocks so the gold was free. Once in a while a piece of gold still had some quartz clinging to it.

February 1st and back.

"We have a good ounce of gold for our January work. Mr. Peterson showed us a place to dig in the water and we dammed it off and made pretty good money. We got half an ounce in about three days work. The place is about to run out now and we have to fight water all the time.

We made a smokehouse out of burlap and smoked twenty-five big suckers. They weren't so hot so I made a live box and we have fresh fish for every supper. The smoked fish were too chewy for us but Joe Garrity thought they were good. He ate the most of them, even wanted us to smoke more.

A while back Glen saw a four point buck just across the creek in the hills. Glen caught a grey fox yesterday.

Warren pulled out and left his partner, Joe, up at the tin shack. Now Joe is around here most every night, makes a pest out of himself. He hangs around for meals. The other night when we gave him a jack rabbit feed he told us to give him another invitation when we got another rabbit and he would enjoy it very much. That same night, Glen caught a big tom cat in a trap by the camp. The next day he cut off a hind leg, dressed it and gave it to Joe and told him he had caught another rabbit. Joe took it and when he came down the next day we asked him if his jack was a little tough. He said, "Yes, it was but it was damn good just the same." Well, from now on I think we will eat all the cats ourselves."

When Glen caught the old traveling tom cat he brought that hind leg back to camp, wrapped it up nice in wax paper and that afternoon we waited for Joe to come by. He usually showed up later in the afternoons and sure enough he came down the trail, gun in hand, cane in the other, out to where we were working. Glen said. "Joe, I got a jack last night and saved a leg for you." Joe really appreciated that, thanked us and packed on up the trail. That evening we were sitting by the camp fire over with Mac and Mr. Landus, the oil men. We had already told them what we had done with the cat. It wasn't long before we heard Joe come down the trail, poking stones with his cane. He came in the huddle and sat down and we talked for a while. When Glen asked, "Joe how was your rabbit?" Joe's exact words were: "Well, I got home late tonight, I flung it in the pan and I don't think I cooked it quite enough, because it was tougher than hell, but it was good just the same." We never cracked a smile or said a word. Joe never did find out what he ate. We were always afraid if he did he might shoot one of us with his rifle.

We had always heard that skunks were good to eat, so we tried one. Glen caught a nice big fat one in one of his traps. He skinned it out good, so not too much odor was left when he brought it back to camp. I took it down to the creek and cleaned all the fat off good, washed it and we had a really dark red carcass to cook. We cooked it a long time, boiled it, threw in some vegetables and we were ready for a feed. It wasn't the best eating, still bright red, and tough as leather. We threw the rest out. That was enough to keep us from eating any more skunks.

Dad Wilson had given us the sourdough starter and he told us how to make bread. It was easy after we got on to it: mix up the flour and water, add the other ingredients, knead it good, put it out on the rock in the sun and let it rise, then put it in our oven. We had perfect loaves of bread and often carried sandwiches or bread and honey, with us when hiking around the hills.

February 18, 1934. Sunday.

"We had a big day today. Glen and I each raked in three dollars. The Fox film outfit has been around here and up to Kernville lately. Last night they put up a dozen tents up by Joe's tin shack, a quarter of a mile up the line. They hired Joe to watch it but last night he was down to our tent until after ten. This morning we were up early and all of us miners were up to Joe's ready to sign up as extras. We all got on okay. The first thing we did was chop limbs and tacked on some timbers and made a pine tree for a background. The name of the picture was "The Gold Rush of 1934". They snapped some shots of an old prospector and his burro. Then all us extras were in the picture. They had us up and down the river in front of the tents at work. Glen and I were shoveling and swinging a pick out in the middle of the river. When that scene was shot they had us tear down the tents and be darned if our neighbor didn't swipe a brand new tent and they never missed it. When we were tearing them down he had his car parked on this side and he wrapped it up and when the crowd wasn't looking he slipped it into his car and got away with it. After that we just helped around. They snapped the burro and old prospector crossing the bridge. The burro was on the bridge about two feet from the top of the water and they tried to back him up and he fell over on his back in the water. He lay on his back with his head sticking out and he would not move till the men pulled him out. Then they ran the scene over.

We had a first class dinner. I found a good shovel they left after it was all over. I went down to Bakersfield yesterday with Peterson and brought back twenty dollars worth of supplies. We got 75 pounds of flour, 40 pounds of corn meal, and 30 pounds of sugar. So, we are pretty well stocked up. I also brought up a batch of grub for Joe Schafer.

Hook Schafer and his wife are our new neighbors. They're from Long Island, New York and have been mining in the north last summer and want us to go in with him next spring and pack back into the mountains of the mother lode country. Since the New Year Glen and I got out nearly two ounces of gold. Last week we didn't do anything. We carried some boards back from the Dutchman's place, two or three miles back in the hills. We used them to build up our tent which made it much better.

The other night Hook Schafer and his wife were coming over to our tent and Mr. Landus was just back of them. When he finished smoking, he blew the ashes out of his pipe. Hook heard that noise and swore it was a wild cat. He had his big flashlight and threw it all over the mountainside trying to spot that cat.

Dad Wilson, Joe, Landers and Schafers were all in our tent last night and we made up a big batch of candy. Dad told us stories of his olden days in the Blue Ridge Mountains country of Carolina. When he was a boy he used to haul moonshine through those mountains late at night so the revenue man wouldn't catch him. Mr. Landers' partner, Mack, came back today. Glen got another fox, making it three grays now. I sat a coon trap in the water up by Joe's tin shack and nearly caught a movie actress in it. They snapped pictures just below it and those girls ran all around in the creek close to my trap."

We were fairly used to seeing movie outfits on the river. Several times coming home from town there would be some small, two-bit outfit shooting a movie along Dad Wilson's place, always some kind of a western. We often sat on the hillside and watched them for a half hour or so. When word got around that Fox film was going to film right by us; we were really excited to hear they wanted all the local miners for extras.

Carrol Lombard and John Bowles were the stars of this show. When we went up the first morning some director told all of us miners what he wanted done. Some cut branches and made a tree in the right place, some painted some large shiny boulders a green color, so as not to reflect the sun, and some made a pole bridge across the creek in one of the narrow places.

The movie set was where the river spread out, probably fifty feet or more wide, over a gravel bar. The water there was from a few inches to maybe a foot deep in the deepest spots. What they wanted was action. There must have been twenty or more of us in the scene. They had us spread out along the creek and when they gave the word, we were all to get busy: some shoveling gravel up, some swinging a pick, some washing gravel in gold pans, anything, just so we were looking for gold. They ran that scene several times. We were wet when it was over and all of us had on our leather boots, big hats, and old clothes.

Carrol Lombard was a really beautiful lady. She was dressed in a fine western outfit with a silver fox fur around her shoulders.

John Bowles was a well dressed gentleman, walking around with directors and they probably had a dozen or more of the other actors at work. On one scene they had me hold a large reflector in the background. I guess it put more light on those acting. They shot different scenes all the time but only one scene where Miss Lombard and John Bowles were in. It was mostly a love scene by the river.

The old prospector with his burro was the best to watch. He was dressed for the part, full beard, old clothes and leading a burro. The little old burro had a pack on his back; about as big as he was, with shovel handles sticking out and some extra gear hanging on the pack. For some reason they wanted him to back up a few feet on the bridge. The bridge was made of three or four logs laid over the creek with boards nailed on top. It was probably three feet wide at the most. When the old prospector tried to back up the burro, he more or less sat down on his hind legs and then rolled off into the water. He wasn't about to get up either, as long as his head was out of the water and he could breathe. The men finally pulled him out, got him on the other side of the river and let him shake himself off. Then they tied the pack back on and reshot the scene.

I asked one of the film company's men what name they were calling the picture and he said, "Gold Rush of 1934" but I never heard of it and it probably wasn't the right name anyway.

They paid us in new one dollar bills and we felt quite rich taking in six dollars for the day besides having a really good dinner. The next morning I went up and looked around and found a good shovel, handle painted green, in the brush where some workman must have left it. I gave Mr. Peterson two dollars for my ride down to Bakersfield for supplies. First thing when I went down was to go to a jewelry man who advertised that he bought gold. I had our gold dust along and he weighed it out on his scales and paid me cash. The exact amount I got I can't remember but it was something over forty dollars. When Roosevelt got into office, one of the things he did was raise the gold standard from $20.67 an ounce up to $35. Almost double, so from then on most of the miners got paid for their work. When I went into a Jap store and started buying, the old Jap really beamed. He asked a lot of questions about our work and how many miners were up on the creek and he wanted me to be sure and come back. Twenty dollars was a big order, probably the biggest he had for some time. We always bought a lot of dried fruit: apples, peaches, apricots, and raisins.

We used a lot of dried apples for apple pies and to eat the way they came from the package. If we ate many dried apples and then drank something, they soon swelled up in our stomach and we felt full. One night Joe was over to our camp just sitting around talking and we got the dried apples out and Joe started eating on them. After he ate a lot of them, we made a batch of cocoa. After Joe drank a large cup of cocoa, the apples started swelling up and when Joe left he was really in pain. We knew what would happen when we kept giving Joe the apples and then the cocoa.

A while back I was down by the river working our hole out for gold when Glen showed up, scared as the devil, talked in a low voice so no one around could hear and said he had just shot a deer up in the woods. They say this was a game preserve, no deer hunting allowed, so we had to be really careful. If one miner knew it, before long it would be all over. Glen had the twenty-two rifle, was checking his traps, and the deer walked out of the brush and stood there. One shot and it fell dead. We waited until late in the afternoon then went up and skinned it out. Took the quarters, other good meat, and we had a shovel along and we buried the rest in the brush.

We had a lot of good meat when we went back to camp. That night we really feasted on steak. How to keep the rest we weren't sure but we had heard somewhere that to keep fresh meat, it was best to put it in bags and bury it in cold water. We did that, cut it all up, put it in some cloth bags and we hid it under some brush in the stream just above our camp. When we wanted some the next day we took a bag out and the meat was spoiled, ended up burying the whole works. We found out putting meat in water isn't the right way to keep it.

February 28 and back.

"Glen caught a coyote this morning. We and the Schafers went across the river into another range of mountains to look for placer but found nothing. We met an old timer camped in the mountains over there. He had been to Alaska, he said he was the discoverer of Nome beach gold and had made thirty dollars and more in a day.

Joe hasn't been down to see us for a long time now. He's either sore or afraid Schafer will be here. Schafers and we went up to Dad Wilson's last night and made fudge.

There are two young boys from North Carolina camped below us. They're around here some. One tells of all his adventures. He says he's been in plenty of jails, reform schools and he steals anything he can."

All kinds of characters come and go, some stay a few days and look the river over, some stay longer and do a lot of digging and really work at mining. One day we could hardly believe what we saw, here came an old man on one peg leg, pushing a wheel barrow with all his possessions in it. We called him Pegleg while he was here. He made his camp below ours, maybe half a mile or so.

I got quite well acquainted with him and would usually go down every day or so to see how he was getting along. He had a wood peg leg, just like you see pirates on ships have. I never asked him how he lost it or where he came from. He used a canvas lean to for shelter, cooked over an open fire place and spent most of his time moving rock and cleaning out cracks. I helped him at times move some big rocks by the bank so he could dig down, scrape out any cracks and he found some gold and he was happy.

From our camp the river dropped in elevation a lot. In places there were big potholes in the rock, some big enough to get down inside. These potholes were formed when the river was really big, thousands of years ago. A rock would stop in one spot and whirl around and start a small basin. In time more rock lodged in the basin and the action of water and whirling rock dug out these giant pot holes. I cleaned out lots of them, once in a while I found color but we knew they had probably been cleaned out many times by the old time prospectors.

As we went downstream we found big deep ponds of water. We always checked them for fish, especially where we could see bottom. I spied a big white fish in one hole, went back and got my willow pole and finally snagged it. It was the biggest fish we had gotten all winter, maybe five pounds or more. We baked it with some vegetables and it made one good meal, but were we ever full. Glen and I have taken lots of trips back up into the mountains. We checked several old mining claims where we found the tin can with the claim papers still inside. When a person stakes a claim he piles a pile of rocks in the middle and his claim extends so many feet each way. Usually there would be evidence left of a hole in the ground which led to a quartz vein. Claim papers were always put in a tin can with a tight lid. We read several old claims but never made a copy of any. All these claims were made with the intent of doing hard rock mining. I took one good picture of Glen reading one of these claims.

Late one afternoon we were in the mountains a long way from camp and a storm was coming up. Clouds looked really dark and we checked our compass and took a course down off the hills that would take us to the river. We knew we could find the road down by the river and we could follow that back. When we got off the mountain we were right in a ghost town. Several old buildings were still standing, not a single place that looked like anyone had lived in for years. The clouds darkened and rains started falling, we got in one of the old houses and holed up there for probably an hour before the storm blew over. The house was littered with trash; some old papers were dated back to the eighteen hundreds. Nothing of value to us, when the rain stopped we got on the road upstream and walked back to our camp. We never did get back to that old settlement to check it out or know what it was called. Old settlements were common to us so we never thought too much of it at the time.

March 7 and back.

"Last Sunday I got a small duck. Dad Wilson cooked it up with dumplings and I took up a pie and we had a feed at his place. I went down and had Marshall weigh the gold dust. We have 415 pennyweights and we're going to send it to the mint pretty soon. Joe stepped on a spike about ten days ago. He acted like a baby over it. He stayed in his shack for nearly a week and never went to see any one. I stopped there one day and he was pretty sore. He didn't ask me in or anything. I guess he expected us to all run up to his place to carry in his wood and water. To hell with him from now on.

Mr. Landus and I made a big raft up the river to fish from. We have it in dock number 1 of Wilson Harbor. We make pies here a lot. I just finished making three lemon pies. Gave one to Schafer and we're taking one over to Landus. He invited us over there for a big stew feed. We're going after turtle pretty soon and have a turtle feed some time.

Glen wrote to several cities trying to find a market for rattlesnake oil. If we can get a good price for it, we're going to Texas to hunt them."

Awhile back I was walking up the trail by the river and looking through the brush I saw five or six ducks in a small pond. I ran all the way up to Dad Wilson's place and borrowed his twelve gauge shot gun. It was a single shot and I took two or three shells and ran all the way back down. I sneaked through the brush real carefully, thinking all the time we would have a big duck feed. I got in range and fired right for the middle of the flock. I could hardly believe it; everyone got up and flew away. The duck I did get later on was with the twenty-two rifle.

We had often talked about what we would do when spring came. Glen came up with the idea there might be a market for rattlesnake oil. How to make the oil, we didn't know, but we had seen ads once in a while about snake oil cures. We killed just a few valley rattlers up and down the river. These valley snakes were really small, seldom over two foot in length with small rattles, and very dark in color. They were just as poisonous, so we always wore leather boots and when the weather was warm, we always had an eye out for them.

We only had one snow storm all winter where the valley was white. It was maybe three or four inches but in a day, it was all melted.

March 11 and back.

"Mr. and Mrs. Schafer pulled out last Thursday on the eighth. Mr. Landus, the Carolina boys and we were all over to help them load up and see them off. That night the Carolina boys and we went up near Joe's shack about twelve o'clock and raised hell. Ott and I stayed in front of the shack to watch for Joe while Glenn and Bill went around near the back. Glen shot the rifle three times to wake Joe and then Bill started screaming, worse than some women. Then Glen shot the gun off some more. We didn't see a sign of Joe. Guess he hid under the covers. We expected to see him the next day go down to the creek and wash out his blankets.

The next day in the morning Joe came down to our tent. Mr. Young and I were here talking. Joe wanted to know what it was we caught in our traps last night. I told him we didn't hear anything or catch anything. Joe claims it was some animal scream, awful piercing as if it was dying. Lately we have been talking about a mountain lion to him and he thinks now that is what it was only he can't account for the shots.

The morning Schafers left, someone got into Mr. Landus' camp and stole his rifle and shot gun. We went up the river fishing after we saw Schafers off and when we came back Landus discovered his loss. That afternoon we found some track above his camp that must have belonged to the thief. Glen compared them and they compared exactly with Mr. Young up at the Rock House. That evening Glen went to Young's to sneak around and try and hear something.

He stayed until they went to sleep but they never mentioned guns. He got by a window, when he first got there, and listened. Then the Misses came out, before they went to bed, and let the dog out and the dog smelled Glen. He beat it up the hillside with the dog after him. They came out with the lantern but they thought it was some animal. After everything quieted down, he sneaked back and got under the bedroom window.

The Carolina boys left today, Zeb Owens and some others came up and got them. Mr. Landus is all hepted up for a turtle feed or rather soup. We have three turtles in our live box now but need a few more. We made a net today but couldn't see any big turtles.

This afternoon Mr. Landus took Glen and me down by the Jack Pot Mine to look at a bank of placer. He couldn't find the place. We went by it a half mile. Then he decided it was back a ways, so we came back and couldn't find it so he decided it was on further. Then we walked down the road a mile and then he said it must be back where we had looked twice before. Again we turned around and when we got back we found the placer where we had looked twice before. The placer wasn't any good, so we headed back to camp."

Mr. Landus and his two partners had been following all kinds of leads on where they might mine, either placer or hard rock. They always told us if they could find the right place that paid out they would give us both jobs. We always had it in the back of our minds that something might develop. Mac had a good car, nice outfit and must have some money for a grub stake. Mr. Landus never found out who stole his guns but there had to be one thief on the river some place. When we left camp, if we didn't have our guns along, we hid them in our beds. Our small bottle with gold dust, we also kept well hidden. Very seldom we left camp without the twenty-two rifle. It was always handy to pick off a quail, cottontail rabbit or occasionally a jack rabbit.

March 16, and back.

"Glen got eight dollars for the furs. That's the second fortune we amassed since we were here. The first was when the movie outfit came along. I met the old Mexican, Vic Gonzales the other day. Glen went up and snapped some pictures of him. Yesterday he gave us a drink of raisin wine.

We had Dad and Joe in for supper last night. We always get Dad to tell of his early experiences. I was up to Dad's place this morning and picked about ten pounds of pinion nuts from the pine cones.

Mac and Bud came up yesterday and today they're moving Mr. Landus up to Kernville where they have leased a claim. They are going to work both placer and quartz. I just happened to think of the two Carolina boys. Ott used to be working in the hole and Bill would come along and sit down on the side of the hole. Then when he got up he would say, "Ott, you all look at the seat of my pants and see if any gold is hanging on." Ott would say, "Oh hush up and get busy doing something."

Glen sent our gold dust to the mint at San Francisco and we are wondering how much we have. Sheepherders are starting to come through. I was working down by the water and I heard the tinkling of small bells. I couldn't figure out what was going on and before long up came a band of sheep, old sheep, lambs, and a few goats mixed in. They kept moving and eating along the way. There was probably a thousand or more in the band. They spread out all along the valley from river to the hillside, right through our camp. At the tail end came a sheepherder with his dogs. The dogs worked all the time, kind of moving the sheep along and keeping them bunched up as much as possible. The sheepherder came along leading a burro with a pack on his back, carrying his camp outfit. They came from some place south and were working north for the summer grazing somewhere in the mountains further up.

That first night after the sheep went through Joe came down to our camp all excited. He found an old ewe sheep that had strayed in the brush and he shot it with his rifle. Then he hot footed it down to tell us. We went up, butchered the sheep, buried the carcass and we had our first taste of mutton. Was it ever tough but we had a good feed.

The next day a truck came down the road and stopped on the flat above and just below our camp. Two men pitched a tent, unloaded a lot of supplies and the truck left, leaving one man who I found out later was the cook for the sheep outfit. He dug out a large hole, lined it with rock and built quite a large fire. His job was to bake bread and do other cooking for all the sheep herders who were coming through in the days ahead. For bread pans he used two large, deep, bowl shaped aluminum or some other kind of metal. One fit on top of the other. They were probably a foot or more in diameter and a foot high when they were put together. He made sourdough bread, after it had raised and was ready to bake; he scraped the fire back, buried the tins in the coals, covered them up with coals and left the bread to bake.

One time when I was up to see him he cut up a loaf and gave me half of it. The crust must have been an inch thick but the bread was really good. I never mentioned to him all the time he was there that we were eating mutton on the house. He must have been there doing the cooking for ten days or longer as each day a new band of sheep trailed north.

Vic Gonzales was one of the most interesting old time Mexican miners we met in the hills. He was up stream maybe a mile or more, and then we had to go to our left up the hills and on one hillside there, Vic had his home and mining gear. He had a couple of tin and canvas shacks hooked together for his home. It was his permanent residence and beside the home he had a large tin roof over poles for shade and a place to work. Some fair sized cottonwood trees were up and down a ditch bank and a small stream came by the place. There had been a spring further up the ditch and not too far below his shacks, but it had dried up completely.

Vic was a hard rock miner. He found a quartz vein by his camp and he was digging and tunneling back into the hill following the gold bearing vein. Under his lean-to he had a large flat rock hollowed out like a basin and above the rock he had gears and a handle on the side to turn another rock around and around on the big rock. He turned the crank by hand and it had been turned a lot for the rock was grooved and hollowed out to several inches deep. When Vic got the quartz rock from his mine, the gold was all through the rock. First he used an iron sledge and pounded the quartz up into small pieces, then he put it on his rock grinder, turned the handle, moved the top rock around and around until the gold was loose from the quartz. He probably used the mercury method to pick up the gold out of the crushed stone. Vic had been there several years and was making a living. He had a big wooded barrel covered up with a tarp. He uncovered that and gave us each a glass of raisin wine. Vic said he buys raisins in 100 pound lots and makes a barrel of wine at a time.

Vic was a true blooded Mexican. He talked in broken English and wore a large black hat. His grey hair and beard had not been trimmed for months. He lived alone with a black hound dog for company.

We got a check from the mint for our gold dust we sent in. Check was for $52.67, they even paid $1.22 for the silver that was mixed with the gold. Most all raw gold carries some silver but it can't be seen. After melting we had two and a quarter ounces of gold but only sixty eight per cent fine, so we were paid accordingly.

April 1, 1934.

"Well, Glen broke camp today. He took a packsack and started out for Flagstaff, Arizona, where he thinks he will get work on a ranch. I'm going to stick around for a while yet and see what turns up. After Glen left I went up town to Kernville and played baseball with them. That was the first time I had a ball in my hands this year. I played left field for eight innings and then caught the last inning to show them that I could catch. The manager, Odeoas, talked to me a few days before and said that the town would get good players a job. He told me a lot more but it all was a lot of hot air because the men he had out today hardly knew how to play. I'm going to Ransburg next Sunday to play with them just for the fun of it. Before Glen left we changed the river channel in front of camp and took out twenty-five pennyweights of gold. We darn near killed ourselves doing it. We had four or five feet of overburden and hundreds of gallons of water to throw out.

The weather has been warming up, trapping has been over for a long time and Glen was getting restless, talked a lot of heading out again. He decided to leave on April first and he had all the necessary items packed in his packsack. He took most of the money as I had the gold dust we had saved up since shipping to the mint. We sent the big rifle and some other things back to Wisconsin. The small rifle I had made a pistol out of it. I cut the barrel off and cut the stock down to fit my hand. It would still shoot but not very straight at any distance. It is easy to pack around and I usually keep it with me in case of rattlesnakes.

April 5, 1934.

"So far this week I only made a dime but I have the river changed off again and I am going to work some more. I've been in the butcher business lately. Last Tuesday I went up to Kernville to practice ball and no one showed up. When I was coming home by Dad Wilson's place, they had a lamb tied up. That night we butchered it. I took a hind quarter and roasted it yesterday. Yesterday Joe caught an old sheep and brought it down here to feed on grass. When it gets so it can travel we will turn it loose. Then when he started for home the second time he came back with a big lamb in his arms. We butchered it last night and passed some around to the neighbors. I just roasted a hind quarter. Thousands of sheep are going by now and they lose some all along."

Everyday a large band of sheep would cover the valley, eating here and there but working north all the time. We find stray sheep up a lot of little valleys or in brushy spots. As each band goes through it picks up the strays from the day before but always seem to leave some along the way.

One Sunday a truck came down our way with two men in it. They were picking up all the strays they could find. When they got a load, they headed back out in a big hurry as they were stealing these sheep and starting a band of their own way over on the other side of the valley. I heard later they had over eighty so far in their new band. So many thousands of sheep went through that the owners would never miss a few hundred. One sheep herder told me they keep so many goats in a herd, when they count the goats, and then they know most of the sheep are there. The goats don't hang together but spread out all through the band. When we butcher a lamb we always bury the carcass. Lamb is really good eating and quite a change from living on wild meat all winter. I had a patch of nice grass close to our tent and the old sheep was right in her glory and when the next band went through she joined and was on her way.

April 16, and back.

"A couple of weeks ago I made about four dollars out in the river but it was awfully hard work alone. Then the river came up and washed out the dam. It kept coming up till now there is about ten times as much water in the river as before.

Last week I moved my camp up by Dad Wilson's. I let him have all of my grub and I'm eating with him. Last Tuesday Dad and I went for a hike about eight miles back into the mountains to look at some old Indian paintings. We found them okay and I took a copy of all the sign language. It looked like a lot of ashes in front of the paintings, so we decided to go back up there and camp for a few days and dig around.

I moved my camp up the next day and then on Thursday, Dad and I lit out early in the morning to go back again. We each carried about thirty pounds. We had our packsacks on our backs, one blanket roll around our necks and our rifles in our hands. We had to take it slow as Dad has the asthma and he would say, "Well, let's stop and blow a while."

We got up to the Dutchman's old place and went over to the spring for water. I was just going to dip down when about ten feet away a big rattlesnake jumped up. Dad cracked it with a stick and laid it out. Then we looked around for more and Dad ran across another small one but it got away under a caved in barn. I skinned the snake and took a couple small steaks off the back for my dinner.

It was after two o'clock when we finally got over the mountains to our camping ground. We camped by a spring down in a deep valley with the Indian paintings just below us. I fried up the rattlesnake and ate it. Dad wouldn't even taste it. It tasted like frog legs and it all contracted into a knot in the frying pan.

The next morning I was up early and had some fresh meat for breakfast before Dad was up. Then we took our shovel and went down to the Indian paintings and dug in front of it. The paintings were up to about ten foot from the ground on a large concave rock. The rock looked as if it had heated and water thrown on it to chip it off. It pointed nearly direct south on a point of a hill overlooking the Kern River valley.

We dug through four feet of ashes in front of the rock but found nothing to indicate the origin of the paintings. I took some samples of the paint. The rest of the day we prospected around but didn't find any color. There is a large stone wall here which is in dispute whether it is a freak of nature or handmade. The next morning on Saturday, we pulled out and hiked home by one o'clock.

I played ball yesterday with Kernville and we reamed some team pretty bad. The manager is more of a wind jammer than a ball player.

I was down to see Peterson at Keysville tonight. He borrowed two dollars from me when he was drunk two weeks ago. He was broke tonight and said he would send it to my home when he got his pay. He came nearly quitting his job and going mining. When he was drunk he said, "When it comes to taking care of the money, then the old lady wears the pants, but when it comes to changing jobs, then I wear the pants." I packed some of my things today and expect to leave in a couple of days."

The snow had started melting in the mountains above us and the Kern River started rising some each day. It was probably from twenty to thirty feet wider in the shallow places than before. I couldn't cross it now by jumping from rock to rock. I took my tent down and made several trips up to Dad Wilson's place with all of my gear. I was glad to have company and Dad told me stories every night about his days in Carolina.

He told me about the old Indian paintings and I was anxious to see them. Dad had found them years before hidden way back in the hills. My first trip up I had some old paper wrapped around some gear so I used three pieces of old paper and made a copy of the figures. It never occurred to me to take fresh paper back up and copy all the paintings on good clean paper.

The old Dutchman's place as it was called was several miles from our camp up in the mountains. An old Dutchman made that his home early in the gold rush days. He had a nice flat place on the side of the mountain to homestead. The remains of an old log house, cabin or shed and other buildings had all rotted down. I could see where they had been, close to a spring with probably an acre or more of cleared land by the buildings. He had fruit trees planted and a few wild apple trees were still in the clearing. Dad never heard where he came from or what became of him, only that he made his home there many years before. Now it was the home for rattlesnakes.

The snake Dad killed was the first big diamondback I had seen in the hills. I skinned the snake, dried the skin good, rubbed it with salt and later on I made a nice big hat band for my big hat. The rattler had nice looking, cream colored, close to white meat. I cut off two long pieces off its back, wrapped them up and told Dad we would fry them up for supper.

The Indian paintings were lower on the mountain and by going up a ways; there in a valley we had a small spring to camp by. Dad told me all he ever heard about the Indian camp that had been there years ago when the Indians lived in the mountains. They made their camp by the rock where they could look out over the valley below. His story went like this: In the valley below and along the river lived another tribe of Indians. These valley Indians grew some crops and when fall came, the tribe from up in the mountains would go down and raid the valley tribe and plunder the crops they had grown.

The concave wall where the paintings were must have been twenty to thirty feet long and about fifteen feet high and dished out in the cliff with the paintings still a good ten feet from the ground. The color of yellow or faded orange still showed up really well. The wall had been dished in, just like a big bowl up against the hillside. We dug down in several places a good four feet and never hit bottom. All we found were ashes or dirt and ashes, so we gave up digging. Close to the cliff were large round boulders that had rolled down thousands of years ago. In several of these were the potholes which were probably worn in the rock by the Indians grinding nuts, corn or something. These pot holes were from a foot to a foot and a half across and up to four to six inches deep. Just below the painted cliff was a rock wall and large stones, piled on top of one another. The brush and undergrowth had them pretty well covered but I was able to tell it was a rock wall. It had to have been made by the Indians for some purpose hundreds of years ago.

Mr. Peterson must have lost my home address because my two dollar loan was never repaid. I probably owed him more than that anyway as he and his wife were very good to us. We often had hitched a ride with him up to Isabella and back and I never thought I would get the two dollars back anyway when I loaned it to him.

The days I spent with Dad Wilson were days full of storytelling time. I took paper and pencil and wrote down a lot of his younger day experiences.

Yarns as told by Dad Wilson

Dad's father lived in the Blue Ridge Mountains back in North Carolina. The closest large town was Hendersonville which was twenty-five miles away. Dad's father was an old Sea Captain. He made his money and then he retired to a small farm in the mountains where Dad was born.

Dad Wilson says, "When I was about fifteen years old the government gave my father a job of making whiskey. Instead of making it, my father used to buy the corn whiskey from the mountain bootleggers and sell that. We lived down in a valley near the foothills and my father was a steady customer of an old bootlegger who lived thirteen miles back in the mountains. After my father showed me the way then I had to drive a team of mules back in the hills every week or so after a barrel of whiskey. I always had an old darkey with me to drive and when it would get dark we would set out and cross the narrow winding roads and late that night we would get up to the moonshiners. Then we would stay that day and that night we would load up our whiskey and start down the mountainside. The old moonshiner always gave the darkey a pint of whiskey to keep him in good humor on his homeward trip. The old darkey would take a drink every so often then he would begin to sing as loud as he could. He had one song he sang all the time, over and over: "We'll All Be There When the Judgment Day Does Come." We were supposed to be quiet because the revenue men were always scouting around. But when the darkey had whiskey, he was beyond control.

The old moonshiner would always make the darkey stay at the house when we went to the still to load up. The first time he took me to his still we started off at dark with the mule team. He showed me where to drive and we drove all around for three hours or more before we got to the still. Then a couple of men loaded us up and we drove the brush and all through rough country until we got back to the ranch early in the morning. The next time I went up, the moonshiner told me he wanted to show me his lay out in the daylight. So, he led me through a corn field, opened a fence gate, went through a patch of timber and there was the still not over a half mile from home. I asked him why in hell he drove me all over when I was here the last time. He said, "You see I weren't shor you were okay then and I can't afford to take no chances no how."

We went over a little knoll and the man said, "Well, we're here." I looked around and I couldn't see a sign of a still. Then he said to follow him. There was a little ditch at the bottom of the knoll covered with overhanging brush. He jumped down into the ditch and I followed him. We crawled on our hands and knees till we came to a tunnel in the hill. We went up and there was his layout with two men working it. They had the tank of mash going and whiskey around in barrels to age. Then he told me he was going to show me how they were fixed for revenue officers. He crawled me for fifty yards up the hillside in another tunnel and beneath an old oak tree we came to a trap door. He opened it and we crawled up right into the tree trunk. There were five or six rifles and a big pile of ammunition.

The revenue officers were thick around there and they had to be because they were thinned out pretty fast. When they went to make a raid, there were always a dozen or more in the bunch.

I knew Old Colonel Jordan who lived back in the mountains. He was a moonshiner and was raided once and he killed a revenue officer. There was a reward put out on him and for several years he was hunted but no sheriff or officer could ever catch him. He rode a big mule through the mountains and had lots of friends, so he could get away. He kept on making whiskey and one night when he took his whiskey down to sell to a buyer, the man had plotted with another man to capture Jordon for the reward money. After they got the liquor unloaded they got Jordon into the house for a little drink and a rest. Then they got to comparing six shooters and they got Jordon to bring out both of his guns for them to look at. When they had his guns, they both put their guns on him and told him to put up his hands. They bound his hands behind his back and then one of them kept guard on him while the other went out to put up Jordan's team. Jordan saw his chance and he dived into his guard, hit him in the stomach, knocked him sprawling and he jumped out the door and ran off into the woods. He got some friends to untie his hands and later took his shotgun and went back to kill the men who had tried to turn him in. He went up to the house and the lady said her husband wasn't home. Old Jordan happened to look by the bed and there was the fellow's boots sticking out. He told him to come out and die like a man. He told him he was going to take him out and shoot him. The woman pleaded so hard that Old Jordan let him off on condition that he give him eight hundred dollars to pay for his load of whiskey and his team. The old fellow sent his wife with Jordon to town and she got the eight hundred. When he counted it over he took out one hundred dollars and handed it to her to pay for a horse that he had killed of theirs.

Later Jordan was finally captured. He was riding down a trail on his big mule, musket in hand, and he ran into a posse of deputies. He raised his musket to fire but they beat him to it and broke his musket with a ball. Then Jordon turned to run and they shot him in the back. He was badly wounded and after he left the hospital he went to jail. He was only in jail a few years when he was paroled out because he was about to die with consumption.

When I was seventeen the revenue officers caught my father for bootlegging. They had him down in the county jail along with lots of other bootleggers. They got wind of me helping my dad run liquor so they put out a warrant for my arrest. There was a reward of twenty-five dollars for every bootlegger and for two weeks straight two deputies came to our house looking for me. They didn't have a warrant to search the house so if I happened to be home my mother wouldn't let them in. Usually I would leave early in the morning and go out hunting and would evade them that way.

Then they got so many bootleggers in jail that the County Judge took pity and gave every bootlegger a pardon. My father got me to come down and get my pardon. I rode a horse with my blankets tied behind because I knew I would have to wait a day or two because there were so many mountaineers there for their pardons. When I got to see the judge I walked up to him and there beside him were the two deputies who had been trying to arrest me. When they saw me they scowled and one said, "Why in hell didn't you leave us arrest you so we could get that twenty-five dollars reward?" The judge looked over at them and then he looked down at me and said, "You didn't want to be arrested by two rough characters as they are, did you?" I said. "No, I didn't."

We had to camp by the County seat for three days. There were nearly two hundred moonshiners who drove in for their pardons. Lots of them drove down in a wagon and brought their families along for the outing. All of them had a big jug of whisky with them for company. Right beside our campground was a tribe of Cherokee Indians. One night all of the moonshiners got drunk and so did the Indians. They all started raising hell; the Indians started up their war dances and yelling, then the moonshiners started to pick on them and the Indians got mad and brought out bows and arrows and muskets. The moonshiners got their arms and they were going to have a war. I was the only sober one among the moonshiners and I had a hell of a time running up and down trying to stop the fight. Finally they put up their guns and quieted down.

There were lots of funny people back in those mountains. There was one man who was drunk a good deal of the time and every time he was drunk, he wanted to preach. When he was in town, often he would get up on some buggy or wagon and start preaching to whoever might be around; sometimes to darkeys, Indians, or whites. One Sunday he was riding horseback with his old clothes on, he came to a church. The congregation was out in front when he rode up and he asked. "What's the matter? Why aren't you in church?" Someone spoke up and said the preacher hadn't showed up yet and it was already after starting time. "Well," the fellow said, "if a preacher is all you need, come right in and we'll start off the services." He went in, staggered up to the pulpit, laid his hat on the Bible stand and they said that he preached a better sermon than the regular preacher could have preached.

Another time this fellow went on a drunk with a school teacher. When they sobered up they found themselves broke and three hundred miles from home. The fellow said to the teacher, "Now you do the praying and I'll do the preaching and we'll pray and preach our way back home." When they got home the fellow was riding a good horse and had three hundred dollars in his pocket. The teacher was so ashamed that she wouldn't tell what he had done.

One day I was back in the mountains talking to an old timer. I had heard that he had some very funny ideas and I sure saw one. While I was talking to him an old man came up to the house and asked him if he had any work for him. The farmer said, no, he hadn't. A little barefoot boy came up to his dad, started pulling on his sleeve, then whispered up, "Hire him Dad, hire him to peg down cow plots." Their cow pasture was on a hillside and to save all the fertilizer the old farmer had his boys cut and sharpen sticks and put one through each fresh cow plot. Then when it dried, they were gathered and carried up to the garden for fertilizer. The old farmer had thirteen children and he didn't allow any of them to wear shoes till they were twelve years old.

One time I was back in the mountains after a load of whiskey. We had it loaded up, ready to go down the mountainside. A fog came up and we got off on the wrong road. We tied the mules to a tree and then the darkey and I went over some hills looking for the road. When we came back for the wagon, we couldn't find it. We were lost in good shape then. The darkey got scared and all he could do was moan and pray. It made me mad to think we were lost and I would cuss. Then the old darkey would say, "Massa Wilson, stead of all the cussing you all had ought to be prayin', 'cause we never will get out of this mess no how."

When morning came we were no better off and all that day we wandered around. We went on top of all the high hills but we couldn't get our bearings. Once the darkey went ahead on top of a high hill, then all at once I heard a yell and down the mountainside came the darkey making twenty feet at a step and jumping clear over the small brush. When he got to me all he could say was, "Car, car, car up there."

I carried a six shooter, the only gun we had, and from then on he wanted to carry it but that was out of the question because he would have shot at everything. Toward evening we ran across an old mountaineer. He said it was twelve miles to where we wanted to get back to. We asked if we could stay all night. The fellow said, "Nope, I got eleven kids and we ain't got room for no more." Then I asked to buy some food. Again he said, "Nope, I hardly got 'nough for myself." Later that night we got back to where we tied our mules and found several mountain families out looking for us with lanterns.

Dad Wilson told about the darkey who went hunting and unexpectedly ran onto a bear. He dropped his gun and climbed a tree. The bear kept walking around trying to get him. The darkey was scared and kept pleading with the bear to go away and let him come down. Each time the darkey said something the bear would growl. Finally the darkey got angry and looked up toward the heavens and said, "God, don't show no favors to either that bar or me and you all gouine to see the damdest bar and nigger fight you ever done seen."

A revenue officer found a small child up in the Blue Ridge Mountains. He asked him where his daddy was. The boy said, "He's making liquor." The officer said he would give him a dollar to lead him to the still. The boy said, "Alright, give me the dollar." The man said, "No, I'll give it to you when I come back." And the boy said, "No sir, Mister, I want the dollar now 'cause you ain't comin' back."

Dad Wilson said a man was kidding him about North Carolina, his home state. He said, "You know how the first man ever got out of North Carolina? It was this way. A man came up from South Carolina with a wagon. It was the first wagon the North Carolina men had seen and one man was so attracted that he followed the wagon back to South Carolina all the time waiting for the big hind wheels to run over the little front wheels."

Then Dad said. "Yes, and you know what that man told us about South Carolina people when he got back? He said he saw some man holding a stick up in a persimmon tree. He thought he was trying to poke out a squirrel. He asked him what he what doing and the man said, "I'm raising pork for the market." The man looked up in the tree and there the man had a pig tied to the end of the stick and was holding it up in the tree so it could eat nuts."

Dad Wilson said, "When I was twenty-three I left North Carolina and went west to Texas. From there I drifted north and joined the cowboys in Wyoming. That was when Wyoming was yet a territory and plenty of toughs still rode the range. I joined up with the U outfit and it wasn't long before I could ride and rope, like the rest of the boys.

We had lots of cattle to herd and our mess wagon travelled over four thousand miles some years. There used to be dozens of us cowboys in the one outfit. The boys were of all nationalities. Most of them gave fictitious names and no one knew anything about each other's past history. As long as a cowboy was honest and upright the rest of the boys would stand by him if he got into trouble. Lots of time Sheriffs or officers would disguise themselves as cowboys and join up with an outfit to locate some criminal. If he happened to find his man the other cowboys would ask the criminal if he wanted to go or not. If the fellow said he would go as it didn't amount to anything, the cowboys wouldn't interfere. But if the fellow said he didn't want to go, then the cowboys would gather around the officer and tell him to start riding and never come back or they would kill him on the spot.

One day I was sitting under a shade tree by the ranch house with the foreman and several other cowboys. A stranger rode up to us and asked for the foreman. Our foreman presented himself and asked what the fellow wanted. The newcomer asked if he could get a job. We looked him over and at first sight we could tell he wasn't a cowboy because he had a brand new outfit from hat to riding gear. Our foreman suspected something, so he said, "No, I got too many men now, got to lay off a few boys when I get up the creek a ways." "Well," said the stranger. "I haven't anyplace to go and I have a good outfit here, so I would like to hang around and work for my board a few days."

The foreman said, "All right, put up your horse and go over and get some dinner." When the newcomer came back he hadn't sat with us five minutes before he said, "Say, you haven't a fellow called Sandy with your group, have you?" Well, here was this fellow Sandy sitting right at his back not three feet away. Our foreman knew this newcomer was an officer, so he said, "No, I haven't seen anyone by that name in this outfit." The fellow said, "I heard he was riding for this outfit, I rode with him a couple of years ago, up in Montana and I wanted to find him again."

After dinner we all laid around a while, never said much, then pretty soon Sandy got up, hollered to the wrangler to bring him his horse. Then he casually said, "Bill relieved me yesterday afternoon on watch so I'll go out now and relieve him." He kept one eye on the officer till he rode over a hill then away he went back into the hills. That night he came back, settled up with the foreman and pulled out. The officer was a greenhorn at his business because if he had kept his mouth shut someone would soon have mentioned Sandy's name. The fellow hung around for a few days then he disappeared.

One winter an outfit next to ours started missing a few cattle over by the mountains. There were seven men camped in a canyon doing some mining and they were suspected. A little sawed off runt said he would get them if they were guilty. He was made a deputy and one day before a big snowstorm he rode in on these men. He asked to stay all night and they let him. That night it snowed hard so he couldn't get out so he said he guessed he would have to stay there for a while. After three or four days the cook on morning said, "We're out of meat boys, got to get some today." The deputy said, "Here, give me a rifle and I'll get some beef." The rest of the boys went out with him and down the canyon to where some steers were. He shot one, then when they were dressing it the deputy said, "Boys, we can get all the meat we want, so we'll only take the best parts." When they finished the deputy said, "Say, we ought to get rid of the carcass, you fellows give me a hand and we'll throw it in the river." Then one of the men gave themselves away when he said, "No, we got a shovel hid over here in the bushes, we just bury them where they lay." A few days later, when the path was open, the deputy drew his guns on the fellows while they were at the table. He marched them four of five miles ahead of him to the main highway where he had a trunk hid with handcuffs. He put on the handcuffs and took them right to the jail.

One time there was another pretty slick officer who had something on our cook. He got our cook spotted then he hung around till all the cowboys rode out. When we came back we found the cook gone. That was the only way he could have gotten the cook, because he knew the cowboys wouldn't let him take their friend.

After the law got away with our Chef, we got in another cook who went by the name of Pat. Well, Pat was a tough case. We couldn't leave him have any liquor or we wouldn't have any meals for a few days. Pat was usually a cranky fellow but he always stood by us boys. One day I was riding a bucking horse out in the corral, chasing some calves around when a stranger came up and when he saw my horse buck he said to Pat, "That fellow doesn't know how to ride that horse." Pat dropped his pans, sprang over the fence to face the stranger and bellowed out, "Oh, he don't, don't he? Well, by God you better go out there and tell him how to do it you dirty piker, and if you don't want to do that, then get the hell off this place you son of a $###@ you." One day a smart aleck young man with his girlfriend rode up and stopped by Pat's grub wagon. He hollered in at Pat, "Say, there cook, can you tell me how far it is three miles down the road?" Pat dropped his dishes, jumped over in the door and hollered out. "Yes, by God I can. It's just as far as you can carry some horse manure in your mouth without frosting." The smart fellow cracked his horse and didn't bother Pat any more.

One spring when I was piloting Pat's grub wagon across the prairie, Pat got hold of a gallon jug of whiskey. I went into camp one day all ready to hit the trail for a new ground and there I found Pat lying in the shadow under his wagon, dead drunk. I got his wagon hitched up, and then I had another cowboy help me get Pat up on his seat. Well, Pat got the reins then I got on my horse and we started out. I looked back after we had gone about ten feet and there was Pat all sprawled out ready to fall off. I knew then that he couldn't drive, so I tied my horse to the wagon and got up on the seat by Pat. The ground was rough,

I had all I could do to handle the team and Pat was determined to fall off. Finally, I stopped, got Pat up on top of the wagon and hogtied him on. I had his feet and arms stretched out and all tied to the corners of the wagon. Several times the wagon hit ditches then old Pat would roll around and yell. After we had gone about five miles, I untied him. I thought, probably he was sober enough to sit up. He got down to the ground then and when I wouldn't hold him, he would sink to the ground like a wet dish rag. Finally he said, "Tie me on again, Wilshum, and we'll ramble on down these plains."

One of the last yarns Dad Wilson told was about the badger and the dog fights the cowboys would pull off. It went like this: They would get a bunch of cowboys together and put an old pot under a tub. They'd have a string tied to the tub; get the dogs all around ready to fight the badger. Then get some stranger to pull the string and tip the tub off the pot.

Dad said one time he was coming up through Oklahoma and the cowboys were putting on a rodeo and to top the day they were going to have a badger fight. The news of the coming fight got downtown and the ladies heard about it. A bunch of ladies known as the Humane Society got wind of it. They got the Chief of Police, along with some deputies and the women rushed down to the rodeo grounds. A crowd was around the tub when they tore through the crowd and the Chief of Police jerked the tub off the pot in front of all the ladies. Then the cowboys yelled and hooted all night.

January 6, 1991.

After fifty-seven years of lying away I got this old diary out and read it. I see that the last time I wrote in it was April 16, 1934. I can't believe that I never finished it as I traveled on, but I was probably too busy, traveling, pan handling, working, riding freights or walking.

I was all packed up in the morning and said good-by to Dad Wilson and started walking. I had a really heavy packsack on my back packed with a small canvas, blanket, change of clothes, canteen, small frying pan, two quart tin bucket to cook in, some dried fruit, rice, oatmeal, cocoa and etc. It was about the fullest I have ever had the pack and it really cut into my shoulders. Finally I put some padding on my shoulders where the straps cut in and that helped a lot. The river was high, so I walked the sand road up to Isabella and there got on the road south to Bakersfield.

I walked most of the forenoon, each step the pack got heavier. At times I would adjust the straps. Then move things around in the pack as hard objects were digging into my back. At noon a man picked me up driving a wreck of an old car. He said he was a prospector and was working up north and somewhere by the edge of a desert.

He showed me some pieces of quartz rock that were yellow with streaks of gold. Some pieces of quartz showed small gold nuggets scattered through it. At the time I could hardly believe he would leave that rock lying on the floorboard under my feet. If it was real gold then he had struck it rich, but if it turned out to be fool's gold, then he had nothing.

He let me off in Bakersfield and the first thing I got was a meal and then went to the place where we had sold dust before. When Glen and I split up he took most of the cash and I took what gold we had on hand. With what I had panned out, I had a nice little bottle of dust.

The buyer weighted out the dust and figured out the amount. I had something over $30 in cash. That seemed like quite a stake for me. I wasn't sure where I was going but I thought maybe I might end up in Texas. I went to a post office and bought a ten dollar money order and mailed it to my friend in Texas. That was Reinhard W. Bippert of LaCaste, Texas. I visited him a few years back and if I did get to his place, I wanted to have some money on hand.

From Bakersfield I headed north, I had on my leather boots, soles full of hobnails, my large cowboy hat with the rattlesnake hatband; pants were always tucked into the boots. Everyone was dressed more or less in rough clothes. No one thought anything about style in those days. I had my money belt under my shirt. I always wore a money belt when traveling, with my traveling money in it and just a little money in my pocket book. I never carried a billfold, just the little pocketbook with a clasp on the top.

I don't remember too much about my trip north but I know it was hot and my pack was heavy. Somewhere along the line I got a freight train and rode it into Sacramento. As soon as I got off that night I headed for some friend's place in Sacramento. These were the folks who at one time lived in Wisconsin.

I had been to their place twice before and now it seemed like homecoming. They were glad to see me again and first thing they gave me a good lunch. I did a lot of work that day, cleaned the chicken coop, mowed the lawn and trimmed some bushes.

From Sacramento I headed north. My mother had sent me the address of her uncle, would be my great uncle in Newport, Oregon. As long as I hadn't been north, I might as well go up and see him. I had over twenty dollars on me and it wasn't costing me much to live, so I wanted to travel some in the northern part of the U.S. I went down to the railroad yards, went in the jungle where the bums hung out, found out when a freight was heading north and before too long I was on my way.

Memory is pretty hazy of my trip to Oregon. I was so used to riding the freights and when they got tiresome; I would get on the roads and hitchhike.

I always had plenty of company on the trains. One young man I remember well. He traveled on the same car as I and we often cooked up a feed down in the jungles while waiting for a train to make up. He smoked cigarettes whenever he could get the makings, rolled his own. Our train stopped in one town and we had a few hours to spend before our freight was to pull out that night.

We went up town to see if we could pick up snipes, so he would have a fresh stock of tobacco. Snipes are the butt ends of cigarettes that are thrown away. He took one side of the street and I the other. It was in the evening and I got the side of the street that the movie house was located on. That's always a good place to find snipes as they throw them away before going into the movie. We both had a lot of fun, hollering across the street when we found an exceptionally good one.

We had our packs with us; all the people on the street knew we were bums. Some would look us over, watch us for a while. I know one man in particular threw two whole cigarettes in the gutter ahead of me. He wanted to see me pick them up, and then listen to our conversation across the street. We put on a pretty good show outside the theater. We each had quite a few butts, along with a few good cigar stubs. My partner would take the tobacco out and then roll his own. He was always happy as a lark after each good hunt.

I got on a freight train and ended up in Spokane. I found my Uncle John living in an upstairs apartment in a residential district. He was glad to see me and I stayed with him two or three days. I had picked up a bad case of poison ivy in some jungle and we went to a drug store and I kept plastered up with poison ivy cream all the time I was there. He was a great horseshoe pitcher and we pitched a lot of games and looked the city over.

I had the schedule of the best freight trains leaving for the east so at eleven o'clock one night, Uncle John took me down to the freight yards. At midnight after the train was made up, I was on it. I had looked the train over good and couldn't find any empty boxcars so I got on top of a freight car and sat on the walkway all night long.

Uncle John had told me he would lend me the money if I wanted to buy a ticket to go home. I wasn't about to waste money when free rides were available. I remember the night well. There was a full moon and everything was lit up. Over one mountain pass after another, probably one of the most scenic rides I ever had, mountains all around and dense forests covering the foothills.

We made stops along the way and I finally got in a boxcar where I could relax. When riding on top of the cars I always had to be on my guard. I might come to a tunnel or snow shed along the way. If that happened, I had to lie flat on my stomach beside the catwalk, hold on with one hand to the walk and with the other hand holding my pack. If it was a fairly long tunnel, the coal smoke and soot would have me choking for fresh air by the time I made it through the tunnel. Often I held a handkerchief or old rag over my nose in order to breathe.

The second morning out the train pulled into Laurel, Montana. This was a division point; trains were torn apart here, and then hooked up again, cars rerouted in all directions. I thought at the time that I had gone far enough east from here I had better catch a train going south. Thought maybe I would go south to Texas and see my friend at LaCaste.

I got the train schedule of the fast freights going south. The older bums in the jungle always knew which train would be local, that is, one that stops at every little town or way station or even might stop way out in the country where there would only be a corral, pick up one or more cars of cattle, and then be on their way. My special freight that went south didn't leave until nearly evening, so I had all day to spend in town.

Between the hobo jungle and town was a large thicket of trees and brush. Back in this thicket I went, found a tree that had fallen over and beside it I hid my packsack by covering it up well with leaves, brush and larger limbs. I took my bearing so I could find it again and after washing off all the coal smoke and soot; I walked up town.

I had all day to spend so I thought I might as well look for some jobs and take in a few cents. I found a nice residential area and went up to a nice looking home, knocked on the door and a very nice middle aged lady came to the door and I started my line, "Mrs. I want to make a few dimes, can I mow your lawn, trim the hedge, wash the windows, rake up the yard, hoe the garden, or any other job you have?" Mrs. Said, "How much do you want to mow the lawn?" I said ten cents would be enough. She looked me over good, asked a few questions and said okay, and got me the lawnmower. All mowers in those days were the push type, some not too sharp either. I went to work and really worked at it, trimmed around the sidewalks, pulled any weeds showing, and then broomed the walk off so everything was really clean. I did such a good job she gave me a quarter then called up a neighbor up the street and lined up another job for me. I worked in that neighborhood until the middle of the afternoon. One person would pass the work on to someone else and I had odd jobs for the day. When anyone asked me how much for the job, I always said ten cents and would usually end up getting from twenty to thirty cents, besides a sandwich or something good to eat.

That was one of the best days I had had for a long time. I know I took in close to two dollars that day. I went downtown to a store, stocked up on grub: can of beans, a big bag of day old rolls, and some other grub, then I went back to the jungle. I found my packsack okay and that evening I got in an empty boxcar and headed south.

I can't remember too much about or just how many days I was on the road south but finally I got off the train in Denver, Colorado. Only one other town I remember. It had its name in big white print up on the mountainside: CASPER.

Denver wasn't too large a city back in 1934. I found a nice home and went up and asked if I could do any work. The folks there were very nice. I did some work for them and then I asked if I could leave my pack there while I looked the city over. It was okay with them, so I put my pack on their back porch and walked uptown. I visited the capitol building, walked all over town, spent most of the day just looking around.

The weather was getting hot and I thought it might be too hot to go south to Texas, maybe I had better work toward home. I left Denver on a nice freight and headed east. Just how many days I was on the road, I don't remember but before long I found myself in St. Louis, Missouri. About the only thing I remember about St. Louis was the ride I got out. I thought I would head for Chicago and see my first cousin, Jessie Holley, who lived in Berwyn, a suburb of Chicago. Also, I could maybe see Helen Nancy O'Malley, who I worked with on Catalina Island last summer and a niece of Miss Grady's.

I got out on the edge of St. Louis and found a truck terminal. I had in mind to hitchhike to Chicago and a truck terminal is a good place to ask for rides. I looked up several truck drivers and asked if any were going toward Chicago. After getting turned down several times I ran across a big lean looking man by a truck and I told him I wanted to go to Chicago. He looked me over from head to foot. I had my heavy hobnailed boots on, a big pack on my back, a cowboy hat and was not too clean looking. He then spied my rattlesnake band on my hat. He said, "Where did you get that hat band?" I said I killed the rattlesnake in the mountains in California, skinned it, ate the meat and made a hat band out of the skin.

He looked at me, used a few cuss words, and then said, "Boy, if you can kill a rattlesnake and eat it, you can ride with me to Chicago, jump in." It was sometime the next forenoon when we drove into Chicago. I walked around the city some then looked up a street car that would go to Berwyn. Jess Holley was surprised when I walked in. It was quite a change to have the use of a bathroom and Jessie really fed me up good. I stayed there two or three days. One of the days I spent looking up Helen O'Malley. Found her home on Garfield Blvd. in Chicago. We had quite a visit about our stay on Catalina.

From Berwyn I got on a street car that took me to the outskirts of the city. I hitchhiked west for Wisconsin and it was about noon the next day when I walked from Mt. Hope the two miles out to the home farm. The folks were sure surprised when I walked in, with all my gear and in good shape.

It must have been some time in June when my trip ended.

Al Kussmaul

Printed in the United States
by Baker & Taylor Publisher Services